FORSYTH PRESBYTERIAN CHURCH
P.O. BOX 539
FORSYTH, GA 31029

Presented to

_____

From

_____

Occasion

_____

Date

_____

Growing in God's Love

A Story Bible

Elizabeth F. Caldwell
and Carol A. Wehrheim, editors

flyaway books

© 2018 Flyaway Books

First edition
Published by Flyaway Books
Louisville, Kentucky

20 21 22 23 24 25 26 27—10 9 8 7 6 5 4 3

Select illustrations produced in partnership with Congregational Ministries Publishing of the Presbyterian Church (U.S.A.).

Darius Gilmont illustrations are copyright © Ariella Verlag/Myriam Halberstam. Published by arrangement with Ariella Verlag, Berlin.

Unless otherwise indicated, illustrations are copyright by illustrator and used by permission.

The stories named "One Hundred Sheep" and "Ten Coins" are adapted from *Who Counts? 100 Sheep, 10 Coins, and 2 Sons* by Amy-Jill Levine and Sandy Eisenberg Sasso and used by permission of Westminster John Knox Press.

Complete story and illustration credits can be found on page 349–53.

Book and cover design by Allison Taylor
Cover illustration by Darius Gilmont
Art Direction: Allison Taylor

Library of Congress Cataloging-in-Publication Data
Names: Caldwell, Elizabeth, 1948- editor. | Wehrheim, Carol A., editor.
Title: Growing in God's love : a story Bible / Elizabeth F. Caldwell and
 Carol A. Wehrheim, editors.
Description: First edition. | Louisville, Kentucky : Flyaway Books, [2018] |
 Includes index.
Identifiers: LCCN 2017043075 (print) | LCCN 2017042864 (ebook) | ISBN
 9780664262914 (printed case : alk. paper) | ISBN 9781611648294 (ebk.)
Subjects: LCSH: Bible stories, English.
Classification: LCC BS551.3 .G77 2018 (ebook) | LCC BS551.3 (print) | DDC
 220.95/05--dc23
LC record available at https://lccn.loc.gov/2017043075

PRINTED IN CHINA

Most Flyaway Books are available at special quantity discounts when purchased in bulk by corporations, organizations, and special-interest groups. For more information, please e-mail SpecialSales@flyawaybooks.com.

Contents

Old Testament

Introduction to the Old Testament   17

Beginning with Creation and God's Promises   19

Rivalries   29

Strong Women and Men   49

Strong Women and Men (cont.)

Prophets 131

The Early Church 287

Listening to Jesus 323

Acknowledgments

My thanks and appreciation go to the publishers, editors, and writers, who, over the years, have taught me the craft of editing. Editing curriculum for Protestant Sunday schools is only learned on the job. The patience and encouragement offered to me was truly filled with God's grace. Somewhere along the way I began to treasure how the church introduces the Bible to the youngest of God's people.

Carol Wehrheim

I am grateful to my parents, Mimi and Bill Caldwell, who gave me a Bible storybook when I was a child. The stories and illustrations engaged my imagination and curiosity, and I wanted to know more. My teachers and colleagues have helped me learn how biblical scholarship continues to add to our understanding of the ways that we hear and respond to the Bible and God's voice speaking in our acts of faith in the world. For their presence and witness in my life, I am thankful.

Lib Caldwell

We are grateful for the support and wise help of our editor at Westminster John Knox Press, David Dobson, and art director, Allison Taylor. Our prayer is that this Bible storybook will be the introduction for many children to a book that becomes a lifelong companion of spiritual nurture and nourishment, and one that they will delight in sharing with the children in their lives as well.

Carol Wehrheim and Lib Caldwell

Introduction

Perhaps you are reading this because you want to share a Bible storybook with a child you know. You may have grown up with one of your own, cherishing the stories and illustrations, wondering about all the things you read about a culture so very far away from your own. Maybe you didn't grow up with a Bible storybook, but you want to learn more about stories from the Bible as you introduce them to your child.

The Bible is less a book of answers than it is an invitation to wrestle with stories and meanings. Engaging a child's imagination by inviting her to ask questions of a story helps her realize it has meaning for her life today. When a child is invited to pause and hear a story and think about how the story is speaking to his life, then he grows up knowing the Bible will be there throughout his life. He learns that the Bible is not an answer book that he will outgrow, but one that he will grow into as he matures.

Reading this Bible storybook is an invitation to you and your child or children to engage in a spiritual practice. As a parent, you look at your phone or your watch and wonder about the time this practice will require and how and when it can fit in to the schedule of a busy family. This practice of reading and wondering about Bible stories requires letting go of *chronos* (clock) time and moving into *kairos* (right or opportune) time. So put aside the attention to the minutes required and move into a space that is God's time. Investing in a child's spiritual formation is an opportunity to grow in faith with your child as, together, you read, hear, imagine, ask questions about, and consider the invitation the story is offering.

The stories included in this Bible storybook have been selected for several reasons. Many are ones that are available in curriculum taught with children in church schools. When you look at the table of contents, you will see that the stories are grouped in sections that address a variety of themes in the Bible. This will help you think about a story that might be appropriate for a particular time in the life of your child. Stories have also been selected because they may help a child with issues that she or he faces in life: at school or at home or in the neighborhood. We all can use help with wisdom from the Bible in learning how to live together as peacemakers, learning how to live with those who are different from us, learning how to love as Jesus did.

These stories reflect the recent thinking and writing from contemporary biblical scholars, so you will see some new interpretations of familiar stories. As you read these stories, you will hear issues that are timeless, ones our children need help facing. Also, the stories have been written and illustrated in a way that we hope will be accessible for differently abled children. The stories use inclusive language for God. It is our hope that children will grow up with names for God that are not limiting but that invite them to engage in their growth in the life of faith by dwelling in the mystery of God who is healer, spirit, shepherd, friend, mother, caregiver, peacemaker, father—all of these things and many more.

Finally, pause with the illustrations. You will see a variety of art. It is our hope that this will help children hear and see the stories in new ways and not be locked into viewing biblical characters in only one way. As with the stories, the illustrations invite wondering, reflection, and conversation.

Take time with these stories. Pause, read, hear, and imagine. Each story ends with three questions: Hear, See, and Act. These invite children to engage the story with their own imaginations and to think about the meaning it has for their lives. Enjoy this time of listening together for the ways that God continues to speak through the Bible and through our lives.

Old
Testament

Introduction to the Old Testament

The Old Testament is like a library of books, with exciting stories, poetry, and wise sayings. There are also some sad stories and many stories that help us remember God's love and care. From the first stories of creation in Genesis to the prophets at the end of this section of the Bible, the stories are about God and God's people. God is present from beginning to end. In Genesis and Exodus, we hear the stories of the first people God called as God's people. These two books along with Leviticus, Numbers, and Deuteronomy make up the Torah. These are books of instruction about living in God's way. Then come thirteen books of stories about God's people. You'll read about Samuel, David, Ruth, Esther, Elijah, Elisha, and many more. Psalms are poetry, and they help us know how to talk to God. The last seventeen books of the Old Testament are words that God gave to the people God called to be prophets.

The Old Testament is also Jewish Scripture, read by Jews and Christians today. The stories were the stories that Jesus learned as a child. They are the stories in the background as he taught and healed. In these stories you meet strong women and men, such as Abraham, Sarah, Isaac, Rebekah, Jacob, and Rachel. But many more strong and faithful people will step in and out of this parade of biblical characters. Listen for surprises in the stories, and learn how God acts in the world, then and even today.

Beginning with Creation and God's Promises

Every culture has a story about how it began. For Christians, this story is told in the first book of the Bible. Genesis starts with two stories of creation. Chapters 1 and 2 in Genesis invite us to think about how God is connected with creation, from the smallest insect to the largest elephant, from the teeniest lichen to the giant redwood tree, even with us. God is the focus of these stories. They do not give us a scientific explanation of how the world came into being, but they do help us understand God's presence in all creation then and now. As you hear these stories, notice the role God plays and the role that humans play in these stories of beginnings.

After the world and all that was in it was created, the writers of the next books told stories about how God made God's self known to the humans whom God had created. Like all people everywhere, they were trying to figure out how to live with one another. Sometimes they were good at it, but often they made mistakes. God wanted them to remember how to live with kindness and care toward one another and toward the earth and all living things. God made promises to them and God wanted them to remember these promises.

An important way that God connects or relates to people—us—is through covenants. A covenant is a promise between God and God's people. God promises to be God, and the people promise to follow in God's ways. In the Old Testament, God's people were the Hebrews. Later, they were called Israelites.

Read about the promises God made to Noah, to Abraham and Sarah, and to the prophet Jeremiah. God's promises then and now help us remember that God is always with us, at the beginning of our lives, in the middle, and at the end.

How God Made Everything

Based on Genesis 1:1–2:4a

Long ago, before telescopes and microscopes, before scientists discovered everything they know today, people told stories about the beginning of the world. This is the story about the beginning of the world that the people of God told. They thought everything God made was beautiful.

At first, it was really hard to see. Water was everywhere. So God made light, the light you see every morning when you wake up. When God saw the light, God said, "It's beautiful!"

Then God moved the water around. Some of it, God spread all over the world. Some of it, God put up in the clouds in the sky for rain. God said, "Water's beautiful, too!"

After that, God put the world's water in the oceans and lakes and rivers. Then the dry ground you walk on appeared. In the ground, God planted grass and trees and everything that grows outside your window and outside everyone's windows.

God made the geranium in the little pot on your windowsill too. God said, "Aren't all these plants beautiful?"

To make sure we all have light, day and night, God made the big sun that you see every day. Then God made the moon and the stars you see when you lie on your back on the ground at night. God said, "Don't you think they're beautiful too?"

Finally, God made all the animals everywhere, the fish and the crabs and the whales in the water, and the birds flying up with the clouds in the sky. God made all the animals around us on the ground. Then God made us, people. God said, "Wow! You're all beautiful."

Then God spoke to us for the first time. God told us who we are and what we should do. God said, "You're all my people in the world I made. I made you just enough like me that you too can see how beautiful everything is. Take care of the world. Keep it beautiful. Keep it just as beautiful as I made it."

Hear: What sound do you hear right now in the world God made?

See: What is your favorite animal? What color is your favorite flower?

Act: What can you do to keep the world as beautiful as God made it?

We Were All Farmers Once

Based on Genesis 2:4b–22

This is another story that God's people told about the beginning of the world. In this story, they wanted to tell us why they were farmers. They wanted to tell us why being farmers kept them alive and why farmers keep everyone alive.

Long ago, God made the very first person who ever lived. God took the best, richest, darkest, thickest soil from the ground. God shaped this soil into someone who looked like you and me. Then God breathed God's own breath into this person. The first person took the first breath ever.

Then, in the same best, richest, darkest, thickest soil that God made the first person from, God planted a big farm. God planted the most beautiful fruit trees and the biggest golden fields of grain. God said to the first farmer, "Be good to the rich soil I made you from. Farm it carefully. Grow the best fields and orchards you can. All your food will come from them, and you'll need food to stay alive."

Pretty soon God thought, *Wait, one farmer can't do all this work alone!* So, from the same best, richest, darkest, thickest soil, God made all the farm animals to help the farmer. God made big oxen to carry loads, sheep and goats to give wool and milk. God even made dogs and cats to keep the farmer company. God decided this was a good time to make all the wild animals, too. So God did.

Pretty soon God thought, *Wait, we need a family! Just one person with all these animals? That will never work!* So God made another person, and then the world had two parents who could start a family and work on their farm together.

Long ago, all families were farmers who grew all the food they ate on their own farms. Today, most families aren't farmers. But here's the thing: all the food your family eats, farmers somewhere have grown for you. Do you know who they are and where their farms are?

Hear: Listen for the sounds your favorite crunchy food makes when you eat it.

See: Look at the different kinds of food in your grocery store. Think about who grew them.

Act: Find out where your food comes from and who grows it. Visit a farm near you and ask what it's like to be a farmer.

When the World Started Over Again

Based on Genesis 6–9

Almost everyone on earth has a story about a time when the world almost ended. Most of these stories are about a huge flood, the hugest flood ever. The people who tell these stories put all their little fears into a story about one great big fear: the end of the world. Here's the Bible story about how the world almost ended and how it began again after a huge and terrible flood.

It rained for days and days. The water rose and rose until it covered everything. Every living thing died—almost. Just one person, Noah, built a boat, a boat so big that there was room for his whole family. Actually, Noah built his boat even bigger than that. He built it so big he could bring a family of every animal along too: dogs and cats, elephants and ants, lions and tigers. Noah even brought spiders and snakes on board. And everyone got along just fine. They were all safe for now.

The big boat floated on the big flood. It seemed like forever for all the families on the boat. Then one day, the sun came out. The clouds disappeared, and the rain stopped. Noah's huge boat came to rest on dry land. Noah opened the windows. When he saw that it was safe, he opened the door. Everyone went bounding out into the new world, running and jumping and scampering in all directions. They found new homes and started new families. They made new lives for themselves.

Then God told them all, "Don't be afraid that the world will end. Don't worry that this will ever happen again. I'm going to make a promise to all of you, to the whole world and to everyone who lives in it. I will keep you safe."

When God made this promise, God was talking to the whole world. God was talking to elephants and ants. God was talking to spiders and snakes. God was talking to pet dogs and pet cats and pet hamsters. God was talking to everyone in Noah's whole family. God was talking to your whole family. God was talking to you.

God said, "Just to remind you of my promise to keep you safe, I'll make the rainbow. When it rains, don't be afraid. Just look for the rainbow."

Hear: What are the sounds you hear when it rains?

See: What colors do you see in the rainbow?

Act: How can you help God make sure that everyone God promised to protect is safe?

Abram and Sarai Find a New Home

Based on Genesis 12:1–4a; 17:1–16

Sometimes families move. They move from one neighborhood to another. They move from one city to another. They even move from one country to another. When families move into one country from another country, we call them immigrants.

That's what Abram and Sarai were: immigrants. They lived in Haran, where their families had always lived. They knew everyone, and everyone knew them. They lived the lives they had always lived, and they did the work their families had always done. They were comfortable in Haran.

Then God came up with a new plan for them.

One day God said to Abram and Sarai, "I want you to move to a new country. I've got a new home for you there. I've got a new life for you. I've got new work for you to do. I want you to live in your new country and work there. Just by living there and doing good, you will make everyone's lives better."

Abram and Sarai must have been worried about moving. It's hard to leave what you know. But they left right away for their new country, the land of Canaan. Like all immigrants, they must have felt strange there at first. They must have felt alone. They must have worried what would happen to them in this new place.

But when they got to their new country, God met them there. God said to them, "I'm going to give you a family. They'll live in this new country and call it their own. They'll make a home for themselves here. Because you're starting a new family in a new land, I'm giving you new names. Abram, you'll now be called Abraham. Sarai, you'll now be called Sarah."

So Abraham and Sarah started all over in their new country, just like many immigrants do today. They had a new place to live. They had new names. They had a new family. And, before too long, they began to feel at home.

Hear: Have you ever heard people who have moved from another country speaking a different language than you do? Do you know the name of their language?

See: Look for those around you who have moved from another country. Ask them where they moved from and what life was like there.

Act: How can you help others feel at home in their new country?

Rivalries

A rivalry between two teams can be fun. But a rivalry between sisters or brothers usually isn't. One of the things that is good to remember about reading stories in the Bible is that these stories are about things we still experience. Families still have things they don't agree on.

Arguments and fights caused by a rivalry between two persons are found in some Old Testament stories. Sometimes it took years for the ones who argued to get back together. And not all stories have a happy ending. When you read about Jacob and Esau, you'll hear a really wild story about what a brother did so he could inherit the wealth of his family. The story about Joseph and his older brothers is a really long story full of all kinds of twists and turns. You'll hear about dreams, hard times and good times, kings and servants. And then there is a sad story about two women who didn't get along, Sarah and Hagar.

But no matter what caused the rivalry, God was with each person. As you read these stories, remember how you feel when you have an argument with someone. Remember what it takes to make up again. Wonder about the people in the story and how they feel, what they experienced, and how God was present with them.

How the Twins Were Born

Based on Genesis 25:19–28

Do you know any twins? Do they look a lot alike or are they quite different? This story is about twins who look very different.

This story starts when Jacob and Esau were zero years old. They weren't even born yet!

Sometimes, before babies are born, they move around inside their mothers. Their mothers can feel them move. Rebekah did.

Rebekah said, "Wow. Things are busy in there. I think I've got two babies, not just one. It feels like they're wrestling with each other inside me right now. I wonder if they'll always wrestle with each other."

Rebekah was right about everything. She was right about the twins and about their wrestling. Esau was born first. He had a lot of red hair, so they called him Esau, because Esau was their word for "red."

Jacob was born second. He stuck out his arm right after Esau was born, like he was still wrestling with Esau. So they called him Jacob, because Jacob was their word for "wrestling."

Esau and Jacob were a lot alike. They were born at the same time. They played together. They grew up in the same family.

But they were also very different. Esau loved getting outside. He liked the outdoors. He liked hiking. He liked hunting and fishing. He brought fish he caught and animals he hunted home to his father, Isaac. Isaac liked Esau a lot.

Jacob liked staying inside. If they had had books and smart phones, which they didn't, he would've read those all day. He made things at home, and he helped his mother cook. Rebekah liked Jacob a lot.

Just as Rebekah had thought, Esau and Jacob wrestled with each other their whole lives. Just like all brothers and sisters who fight, Esau and Jacob did too.

Once, when they got older, something big happened that made them really, really mad at each other. That's what happens in the next story.

Hear: What do you think Esau and Jacob said to each other when they were growing up?

See: How do you think these twins looked alike? How were they different?

Act: Why do you think brothers and sisters, and friends, sometimes fight with each other?

Esau and Jacob Both Want Their Share

Based on Genesis 27:1–29

What's the maddest you've ever been at your brother or sister or a friend? All sisters and brothers, and even best friends, get mad at each other sometimes. It's not just you. Here's the Bible story of two brothers who got super mad at each other, and what happened when they did.

Esau and Jacob were twins. But when they were born, Esau was born just a little bit before Jacob. In those days, the rules said that the oldest brother got most of his father's money when his father died. When their father, Isaac, was old and blind, he decided to give almost all his money to Esau, just because he was a tiny little bit older. That's what the rules said.

"That's not fair," Jacob said.

His mother, Rebekah, agreed. "That's not fair," she said.

So they figured out a plan they thought was more fair, a plan to make sure that Jacob got some of Isaac's money too. This was their plan: Jacob would pretend to be his brother, Esau.

When his brother, Esau, was out hunting, Jacob dressed up like Esau. He put lamb's wool on his arms so that he'd feel like his hairy brother. He put on Esau's clothes so that he would smell like his brother. Then Jacob went to his father, Isaac, who could hardly see anymore. Isaac felt Jacob and smelled him, and he thought Jacob was Esau. So Isaac signed most of his money over to Jacob.

When Esau found out, he was really mad. He said, "Those aren't the rules!"

Who do you think was right, Esau or Jacob? When brothers and sisters get really mad at each other, they always think it's the other person's fault, right? Who do you think was right this time?

Esau was so mad he wanted to kill his brother. Jacob was so scared he ran away from home. They were brothers who grew up together, but now they were far apart. They would not see each other or talk to each other for years and years.

Hear: What do you think Esau and Jacob said to each other when they were both so mad?

See: How do you think Jacob looked when he dressed up like Esau?

Act: What would you do if you were Jacob? What would you do if you were Esau?

When Things Get Really Scary

Based on Genesis 32:22–32

Sometimes, everything gets scary!

After living away from home for many years, Jacob missed his brother, Esau, more and more. Finally, he decided to go home to see Esau again. But Jacob was scared to go home. Esau got wicked mad when Jacob left home with their father Isaac's money. Jacob was afraid his brother would still be mad.

On his way home to see his brother, something even scarier happened. One night, Jacob took his whole family across the last river they had to cross before they got home. Then he sat down in the dark by the river to think.

Nearby in the dark, someone moved. Jacob jumped. Who was it? His brother, Esau? A ghost? A stranger? He couldn't tell in the dark.

Suddenly, a mysterious stranger grabbed Jacob, and Jacob wrestled with him. They wrestled and wrestled into the night. Jacob couldn't see anything. He didn't know what to do.

When he was more afraid than he could ever remember, Jacob heard a voice. He didn't know where it came from. The voice said, "Let go!"

"Help me," Jacob said.

"What's your name?" asked the voice.

"Jacob," he said.

And then the voice surprised Jacob. "I'll give you a new name," the voice said. "Your new name will remind you that God is always with you. No matter what happens. No matter how afraid you get. Even when you can't see and don't know what to do. God will be there. Your name will be Israel."

And then everything disappeared. The voice was silent. The stranger was gone. Jacob sat down by himself in the dark.

When the sun finally rose, Jacob got up and walked away from the river to meet his family. He was limping from wrestling with the stranger, but he had a new name. And his name reminded him that God would be there when everything gets really scary. Even in the dark. Even when he didn't know what to do.

Now he wanted to see his family again more than ever. And he wanted, finally, to meet his brother, Esau. *Now I have the courage*, he thought, *to meet Esau again.*

Hear: What do you think Jacob heard that night?

See: When have you felt scared? Perhaps you couldn't see or you didn't know what to do.

Act: Remember God is with you even when you are scared. What can you do to have courage?

How Esau and Jacob Got Over It

Based on Genesis 32–33

It's not easy to stop being mad at someone if they did something mean to you. It's really hard. Jacob and Esau knew what it was like to get over a fight.

Jacob and his family left the river where he wrestled with the mysterious stranger and got a new name. Soon Jacob saw his brother, Esau.

Esau brought all his friends with him. His friends were four hundred strong men who knew Esau well and would fight for him.

But Jacob had a new name. He thought he also had new courage to meet his brother. But when he saw Esau and his strong friends, Jacob got scared all over again. He gathered his whole family together to protect them. He walked ahead of them to meet his brother, Esau. He bowed down to the ground seven times. He wanted to show Esau that he would do anything to make things right again.

Esau could have done anything. He could have sent his four hundred strong friends to fight Jacob. He could have taught Jacob a lesson. He could have gotten even. He could have paid Jacob back for taking their father's money. But he didn't.

Esau ran to meet Jacob, wrapped his arms around him, kissed him, and cried. He was that happy. "Who are all these people behind you?" Esau asked Jacob.

"They're my new family," Jacob said. "And I've brought you a huge present to make up for everything."

But Esau was just happy to see his brother again. "I've got enough," Esau said. "You don't owe me anything. I can't believe how good it is to see you again."

Jacob was happy to see Esau, too. He now knew that they could be brothers again. Esau had put their old fight behind him. Jacob was so happy, he said, "When you wrapped your arms around me, it felt just like God wrapping God's arms around me. I want you to take my present anyway." So Esau did.

The two brothers who had a big fight, that they thought would never end, got over it. Nobody did anything grand, really. They just decided to start over because they were brothers. And they wanted to be brothers again.

Hear: What did Esau's voice sound like when he first spoke to his brother, Jacob?

See: What did Jacob's face look like when he saw his brother, Esau, again? What did Esau's face look like when he saw his brother, Jacob?

Act: What can you do to make up with your sister or brother or best friend after you get mad at each other?

Joseph and His Brothers

Based on Genesis 37:1–36

Every family has stories they like to tell over and over again. This story and the next two are ones that God's people have passed down for many years. They tell the story of Joseph and his brothers.

Jacob and his family lived in Canaan. It was the land God promised Abraham and Isaac. In Canaan, Jacob's twelve sons looked after the family's sheep and goats. Of all his sons, Jacob loved Joseph the most. Jacob gave Joseph a fancy long-sleeved robe that could be worn only if you weren't working in the fields. The other brothers were jealous when they saw Joseph wearing this robe from their father.

One night, Joseph dreamed he and his brothers were working in a wheat field. The next day he told his brothers, "We were tying the wheat together. My wheat stood up tall. Your wheat bowed down to my wheat."

"Do you think you will be king over us?" they asked.

Another night Joseph dreamed that the sun, moon, and eleven stars bowed down to him. He told his family about this dream. His father said, "Do you really think your mother and I are going to bow down to you?"

One day Joseph's brothers were with the sheep far from home. Jacob sent Joseph to see how they were doing.

When his brothers saw him coming in his fancy robe, they remembered Joseph's dreams. They didn't want Joseph, his dreams, or his special robe around anymore. They said to each other, "Let's get rid of him."

But Reuben, the oldest, said, "But we are not going to kill him!"

The brothers grabbed Joseph, tore off his special robe, and threw him into an empty well. They weren't sure what to do with him. Then they saw a group of traders on camels coming to them. That gave Judah an idea.

"Let's sell Joseph to the traders," Judah said. "They will take him far away from us!"

All the brothers thought it was a great idea. The traders paid for Joseph and took him to Egypt. With Joseph gone, the brothers thought they would be happy.

The brothers knew their father would be worried. They took Joseph's special robe and rubbed it in the dirt. They took the robe to their father. He cried, "It is Joseph's robe. A wild animal has attacked him."

Jacob cried and cried. No matter what his sons did, Jacob was sad. He was sadder than they had ever seen him. He said he would never be happy again.

Hear: What do you think the brothers said about Joseph when he wasn't around?

See: If you could draw Joseph's special robe, what would it look like?

Act: Do you ever feel angry or jealous because someone has something that you don't have? What do you do about that?

Joseph Helps Out in Egypt

Based on Genesis 39–41

Have you ever had a dream that you remembered after you woke up? Maybe you wondered why you had that dream. Joseph was really good at helping people understand their dreams.

When Joseph's brothers threw him into the empty well, he thought, *What have I done to deserve this?* It was even worse when they sold him to the traders.

In Egypt, Joseph was sold to Potiphar, the assistant to Pharaoh. Joseph worked hard. He became Potiphar's assistant. He was in charge of Potiphar's whole house. Even though he was far from his family, Joseph knew God was with him.

One day, Potiphar's wife said to Joseph, "I'm very lonely. Will you be my friend?"

Joseph didn't think that was a good idea. He said, "No."

Potiphar's wife was angry. She told Potiphar that Joseph hurt her. Potiphar had him thrown in jail.

In jail, Joseph was lonely. But he knew that God was with him. The jailer noticed how smart Joseph was and gave him jobs to help around the jail. Then he became the assistant to the jailer. Finally, Joseph was put in charge of all the prisoners!

One day, the head baker and wine maker made Pharaoh angry. They were sent to jail. That night they each had a dream. They didn't know the meaning of their dreams. Joseph told them, "Dreams belong to God. Tell me your dreams."

Joseph told the wine maker that his dream meant that he would be out of jail soon. "Please remember me, and help me get out of jail," Joseph said to him.

When the wine maker got out of jail, he forgot about Joseph.

Two years later, Pharaoh had a dream. He asked the smartest people in all Egypt about it. No one could tell him what his dream meant.

Then the wine maker remembered Joseph. He told Pharaoh about him. Pharaoh sent for Joseph. He said, "In my dream I was standing next to the Nile River. Suddenly, seven fat cows came out of the river. They were eating grass, when seven skinny, sick-looking cows came out of the river. The skinny cows walked to the fat cows and ate them in one bite! And they still looked skinny."

"Pharaoh," said Joseph, "God is telling you what will happen. For seven years the crops and animals in Egypt will be healthy. There will be plenty of food. But after seven years, all the crops and animals will die, and there will be no food."

Pharaoh was amazed at how Joseph helped him understand his dream. He gave Joseph a special job. Joseph became Pharaoh's assistant. He helped Egypt store food so that they would have enough to eat in the seven years when nothing would grow.

Hear: Why do you think Joseph could understand dreams when no one else could?

See: Close your eyes and try and remember a dream you have had. What do you see or hear? What do you think it meant?

Act: Have you ever seen someone who needed help? What did you do? Do you have special talents that could help people in need?

Joseph Helps His Brothers

Based on Genesis 42:1–2; 44:1–5, 16–46:7

Have you ever had a problem that needed solving but you weren't sure what to do? This happened to Joseph's family when they needed food to eat and food for their animals.

Canaan, where Jacob lived with his sons, did not have enough food. Jacob was worried about his family. He heard that Egypt had food, so he sent ten of his sons to buy food there. After losing Joseph, Jacob didn't want to lose his youngest son, Benjamin. So Benjamin stayed at home.

When Joseph's brothers arrived in Egypt, they went to buy food. Joseph was there, but they didn't know him. They hadn't seen him in a really long time. Joseph recognized his brothers, but he pretended he didn't know them. He said, "You must be spies. Why else would you come to Egypt?"

His brothers were shocked. They said, "We're not spies. We're just brothers who are trying to help our family. There is no food in Canaan. We are twelve brothers. Our youngest is home with our father and one brother is gone."

Joseph agreed to let them go. He told them, "I'll let you go home, but one of you has to stay in Egypt. When you return with your youngest brother, then I'll let you all be together." So one of the brothers, Simeon, stayed in Egypt.

When they returned to Canaan, Reuben told Jacob what happened. Jacob didn't want to let Benjamin go to Egypt. He still missed Joseph. He was worried about Simeon, who was still in Egypt. But the family needed food.

When the brothers arrived in Egypt, they met with Joseph again. Joseph asked his brothers, "Is your father still alive?"

When they said yes, he couldn't pretend that he didn't know them any longer. "It's me, your brother Joseph!" he said. They stared at their missing brother.

"Don't be afraid," said Joseph, "God has protected me so that I could help our family! I'm Pharaoh's assistant. I can make sure our family is safe and happy. Return to our father and bring him and everyone to Egypt. I'll give you land, houses, and plenty of food!"

The brothers told Jacob that Joseph was still alive. When he knew that his family would be together again, he was happier than he had ever been.

On the way to Egypt, God spoke to Jacob, "Don't be afraid to go to Egypt. I will make you a great people there."

When Jacob and all his family arrived in Egypt, they were given everything Joseph promised. Their family grew, and they were happy.

Hear: Why do you think Joseph didn't tell his brothers who he was right away?

See: Why didn't the brothers recognize Joseph?

Act: Have you ever been afraid for your family? Talk to your family about what frightens you, and see how you can work together.

A Family with a Big Disagreement

Based on Genesis 16:1–16

Families come in all shapes and sizes. Families can have one parent or two parents. In the Bible, and in some places in the world today, families can even have three parents, or more. The family in this story had three parents, Abraham, Sarah, and Hagar. In some families, whatever their shape or size, parents have a hard time getting along. That's what happened in this family.

Sarah was Abraham's first wife, but she had no children. She was sad and upset about this. Hagar, Sarah's servant and Abraham's second wife, got pregnant. She knew she'd have a child soon. She was very excited. She was so excited that she made Sarah feel even worse. Hagar got more and more excited about herself and about her baby on the way. She cared less and less about Sarah.

This made Sarah even more upset. She felt that Hagar should respect her, not make her miserable, since Sarah was Abraham's first wife and Hagar was her servant. Sarah felt Hagar treated her badly, so she treated Hagar badly back. Sarah made life awful for Hagar. She did everything she could to make Hagar miserable.

Finally, Hagar had enough. She left home. She didn't know where to go, but she couldn't stay. Tired and sad, Hagar stopped by a spring in the desert.

In this most unlikely place, God found her.

God asked, "Hagar, what are you doing here? Where are you going?"

"I'm running away," said Hagar. "Sarah's making life too hard for me at home."

"You'll be okay," God said. "Before long, you'll have a son. You'll call him Ishmael, which means 'I've heard you.' I'll give you a big family, and I'll protect you."

Hagar knew God had seen her and would be with her. She called God, *El Roi*, "God who sees." Then she went back home to her family.

Hear: How might God speak to us when we're afraid and in trouble?

See: How do you think Hagar looked when she left home?

Act: What can you do when you know people in your family are upset with one another?

A Family Changes Its Shape

Based on Genesis 21:8–21

What happens when a family changes? Perhaps a baby arrives, or a grandparent comes to live with you. Usually the whole family changes. That happened to the family of Abraham, Sarah, and Hagar.

When Hagar returned to her family, Sarah, Abraham's first wife, also got pregnant. She gave birth to a son, and she named him Isaac. Now Sarah, too, had a son. She was just as excited about Isaac as Hagar was about her son, Ishmael. The boys were brothers. They played together.

You might think that things were back to normal. But they weren't. Sarah never got over the pain she thought Hagar had caused her. She was still afraid Hagar would become more important in the family than she was. She was afraid Ishmael would become more important than her own son, Isaac. She just couldn't live with Hagar and Ishmael anymore.

So the family split up. Everyone was unhappy.

Sarah was upset. She felt that she and her son, Isaac, had been mistreated.

Abraham was upset because Hagar and Ishmael were leaving. He got up early

to see them off. He gave them food and water for their trip. He put Ishmael in Hagar's arms, and he said his last good-byes.

Hagar was most upset of all. She had nowhere to go. She walked into the desert nearby. She sat down with her son, Ishmael, near a small bush for shade. She began to cry. She didn't know what to do.

But God found her again, just when Hagar needed God most. God heard them crying. God said, "Don't be afraid. There's a well nearby with cool water to drink. You'll be okay. Ishmael will be fine. He'll start a big, new family. You'll have a new home and a new family."

And that's just what happened. Ishmael grew up to be a strong young man. He knew every inch of their new home in the desert. He married a woman from Egypt, and they started their own family in their new desert home.

Sometimes families change their shape, just like this one. When that happens, it is hard for everyone. But God is there to help people make it through.

Hear: How do you think God speaks to you when you are afraid like Hagar was?

See: When Hagar saw the well, what do you think she thought?

Act: Families change when babies are born or adopted, when people are sick, and when parents divorce or get married. How can you be a friend to others whose families are changing?

Strong Women and Men

People sometimes think that the Old Testament stories are all about men. Wrong! Strong, faithful women are all over the Old Testament. They left their homes for new lands. They protected others. They spoke out against evil. They were leaders. God chose them to show others how to follow in God's ways.

We meet many of these women as wives and mothers: Sarah, Rebekah, Rachel, and Leah. These were important and traditional roles for women in the Israelite culture. In those roles they took care of the home, and their children grew up to be leaders for the people. You'll also meet Miriam, Moses' sister, who saved his life. Much later, she helped him lead the Israelites out of slavery in Egypt into freedom as they journeyed into the land promised to them by God. You'll meet wise women like Ruth and Naomi and Deborah, who was a judge. The stories of Vashti and Esther remind us of the important role of women as voices of justice in the culture. And there are others whom God used in God's plan for helping people remember God's commandments.

The strong men in the Old Testament aren't always grown men. In these stories, you meet boys, teenagers, and old men, but God calls each one to an important task. Some are strong in body, and others are filled with wisdom. As you hear the stories of Abraham and Moses, Joshua and Jacob and Samuel, think about their strength. Remember the ways that God called them as leaders for God's people.

When you read these stories, remember that they were written a very long time ago. Some of them may sound strange to you, such as God asking Abraham to sacrifice his son. Other stories make us wonder why women like Ruth and Naomi needed help to live on their own. All the strong women and men in these stories want to live in God's ways and be faithful to God. Their stories remind us that God is always with us, then and today.

God Made Sarah Laugh

Based on Genesis 18:1–15; 21:1–7

Do you remember the last time you laughed so hard that your whole body shook? Listen to this story about Sarah's deep belly laugh.

Sarah and Abraham had been traveling a long time. They stopped and set up their tents. The bright afternoon sun was hot. Abraham was sitting under the shade of the big trees when he spotted three visitors. He ran to greet them. Abraham said to them, "Come rest in the shade of my tree. I will bring water to wash your feet. I will bring you a meal to make you stronger for your journey."

The visitors said that they had a message for Sarah. Abraham ran to her, "Use the best flour we have and bake something delicious for our visitors!" Sarah began to knead the dough. Then Abraham ran to the place where the cattle were kept and took the best one from the herd to his servant. "Prepare the best calf and make a delicious meal for our visitors!" The servant quickly stoked the fire.

Abraham gathered milk and butter. When the bread was baked and the meat was cooked, Abraham served their visitors. Sarah took a deep breath and listened from inside the tent as the visitors ate. She heard them ask, "Where is Sarah?" Abraham replied, "Sarah is right here in the tent!"

Sarah was about to poke her head out to say hello when she heard the visitor say, "I will come back to see you and Sarah in one year. And Sarah will have a son."

A loud laugh burst from deep in Sarah's belly! "How in the world could I have a baby? My old body can't have a baby!"

God spoke through the visitor. "Why did you laugh? What if God could make this promise come true? In one year, I'll return. Sarah will have a son."

And do you know what? Sarah's baby was born when she was very old. Sarah held her baby close. She looked into his beautiful face. She said, "God made me laugh. I believed this day would never come, but now you're here. I will call you Isaac because it means "laughter." I want to remember how I laughed forever!"

Hear: Why do you think Sarah laughed? What did her laugh sound like?

See: What do you think Sarah's baby, Isaac, looked like?

Act: How will you keep your promises the way God kept the promise to Sarah?

God Tugs at Rebekah's Heart

Based on Genesis 24:1–67

How do you welcome guests to your home? Do you invite them to sit down? Do you offer something to drink or eat? Listen for how Rebekah and her family welcomed a stranger.

Rebekah lived with her family in a city. Each night, before dinner, it was her job to get water from the city well. One night Rebekah went to the well with other women from the city. She carried her big water jar on her shoulders. After she filled her jar with water, she saw a stranger praying to God. The man looked up from his prayer and saw Rebekah. "Please," he asked, "may I have a sip of your water?"

"Of course!" said Rebekah kindly. "Drink all you want, and I will go and get water for your camels too!"

Rebekah ran back to the well. She filled her jar again and again until every animal had water. Then Rebekah invited the stranger to join her family for dinner.

Before they ate, the man said, "I have something amazing to tell you! I work for a man called Abraham. He is part of your family. Abraham and his wife Sarah followed God far from here. When they were very old, they had a baby named Isaac. Now Isaac is all grown up. Abraham sent me here to find someone for Isaac to marry. I was asking for God's help at the well. That's when I saw Rebekah. I know that she is the one for Isaac!"

Rebekah's family thought about how far away Rebekah would be if she agreed to marry Isaac. But Rebekah's family felt God tugging on their hearts. They agreed that God was calling Rebekah to marry Isaac.

The man begged the family to send Rebekah with him the very next day. Rebekah's family said, "This is a big decision, and only Rebekah can decide."

So they called Rebekah and asked her, "Do you want to go with this man? Do you want to marry Isaac?"

Rebekah thought about the journey she would take. Rebekah wondered what this man called Isaac was like. But Rebekah felt God tugging at her heart. She said, "Yes. I will go."

Early the next morning Rebekah began her long journey to her new home. She was riding a camel when she saw a man walking in the fields. "Who is that man?" she asked.

"That man is Isaac!" The man who worked for Abraham introduced Rebekah to Isaac. Then he told Isaac everything that had happened. Isaac married Rebekah, and he loved her. Rebekah was glad God had tugged on her heart. She loved Isaac. They comforted each other when they were sad. They cared for each other as they grew old.

Hear: How does God talk to us without using words?

See: How did Rebekah's family welcome the man who worked for Abraham?

Act: Talk with your family about inviting someone to eat with you. What will you need to do to get ready for your guests?

Two Sisters: Leah and Rachel

Based on Genesis 29:1–30; 30:22–24

In our Bible stories, the world was not as crowded with people as it is today. In the Bible, God's people needed to grow their families bigger and stronger. In the Bible, even grown-ups didn't make decisions all by themselves. Their parents had a lot to say about whom they married and where they lived.

This is the story of two sisters, Leah and Rachel. Their father, Laban, chose the person they would marry. He chose someone from his own family so that his family could grow bigger and stronger. He also decided Leah and Rachel would marry the same person. It wasn't unusual in those days for a man to have more than one wife at a time.

A man named Jacob (he was the son of Isaac and Rebekah from the last story) was traveling far from his home, looking for some of his family. Along the way, he stopped at a well to talk to the shepherds there. "Do any of you know Laban? He is my uncle," he asked.

The shepherds answered, "Yes! Laban lives nearby. Look, here comes his daughter Rachel."

Jacob turned and saw Rachel leading her sheep to the well. Jacob was so happy to see Rachel that he kissed her and started to cry. Jacob stayed with Rachel's family and worked hard for his uncle Laban. He wanted to marry Rachel.

Laban was happy Jacob wanted to marry Rachel. He told him, "You can marry Rachel. But

you have to marry Leah first, because she is my oldest daughter."

After Jacob and Leah were married, Jacob married Rachel. The two sisters shared Jacob.

Jacob loved Rachel the most. This made Leah feel sad and alone. When it was time to grow their family, Leah had many babies. Rachel was sad because she didn't have a baby, not even one. She prayed to God for help.

After waiting for a long time, Rachel had a baby too. She named him Joseph. More time passed, and their family grew. They both had more babies. So did their servants. Their lives together weren't always easy, but their family did grow big and strong. They had twelve children who would someday have families and whole tribes of their own.

Hear: What did Rachel and Leah have to say to each other so that everyone could get along?

See: When you see someone who has something you really need, how do you feel? When you see someone sad, what do you do?

Act: If you get married someday, you might pick someone you love. You might choose someone because together, you make a great team. Ask someone you know who is married what they like most about the person they love.

Miriam Hides Moses

Based on Exodus 2:1–10

The Hebrews living in his nation
Grew and grew in population.
Selfish Pharaoh, so very cruel,
Wrote a truly awful rule:

"Because you are too big a crowd,
No more baby boys allowed!"
One Hebrew family, full of joy,
Had just welcomed a baby boy.

Mother took some grass and leaves,
And made a basket to set in the reeds.
She put her baby snug inside,
And took him to the riverside.

Miriam found a spot to hide.
She wouldn't leave her brother's side.
Then Pharaoh's daughter came to bathe
And saw the basket in the waves.

Miriam saw the princess meant no harm,
As she rocked the baby in her arms.
"Shall I get a nurse perhaps?
To care for the baby on your lap?"

Pharaoh's daughter answered, "Please!"
So Miriam ran through the trees.
When mother came to where they were,
The Pharaoh's daughter hired her to care.

One day, when baby boy was grown,
Mother walked him to Pharaoh's throne.
The princess spoke aloud and said,
"I found him in the riverbed,

So Moses is to be his name.
And I will love him all the same,
As though this boy were borne to me,
Adopted now to royalty."

Hear: Miriam had to be very quiet when she was hiding by the river. Be quiet and listen for a moment. What do you hear?

See: Miriam waits by the water's edge to see what would happen to her baby brother. When was a time you watched or waited patiently? What happened next?

Act: In this story, the Pharaoh felt the Egyptians were more important than the Hebrews. How can we make sure everyone feels important?

Miriam at the Reed Sea

Based on Exodus 15:20–21

The people of the Lord sang joyously in celebration,
Delighted that the Lord had saved the Israelite nation.

For God had led them safely to the Reed Sea's other side,
Washing up their enemies within the crashing tide.

Finally they triumphed! They left that awful land!
And so the prophet Miriam took tambourine in hand.

All the women joined her. They grabbed their tambourines.
They danced in praise together, and Miriam would sing:

"Sing to the Lord who triumphed so gloriously for thee!
Horse and rider Lord has thrown into the stormy sea!"

Hear: How do you think the music sounded when Miriam sang?

See: Have you ever seen a group of people dance together in a show or on a stage? How did watching them make you feel? Did you join in?

Act: Miriam sings and dances to celebrate a special day. How do you celebrate when something good has happened? What are your favorite ways to celebrate special times with family and friends?

Leaving Moab

Based on Ruth 1:1–19a

Have you ever moved to a place where you didn't know anyone? If not, what do you think it would be like to live among strangers? Ruth moved from her home in Moab to a new country.

The land of Judah had no rain, no food. Elimelech took his wife Naomi and his sons Mahlon and Chilion to Moab where there was rain and food. After a few years, Elimelech died. Naomi lived in Moab alone with her sons. They married Orpah and Ruth, Moabite women. Ten years later, her sons died. Now Naomi was alone with her daughters-in-law.

Naomi heard that Judah had rain and food again. She decided to return to her hometown, Bethlehem. She, Orpah, and Ruth started the long walk to Bethlehem.

"Wait," said Naomi, "you each should go back to your mother's house. You have been faithful and good to me. May God give you husbands and children."

Orpah and Ruth hugged Naomi and cried. "We will go with you," they said.

"No, I can't do anything to help you," said Naomi.

Orpah finally did what Naomi said. She started walking back to Moab and her mother's house. But Ruth was determined to stay with Naomi. She paid no

attention to Naomi's instructions. Instead she said, "I will go where you go. I will live where you live. Your people will be my people. Your God will be my God. I will never leave you as long as you live."

Naomi could tell that Ruth would not change her mind. Ruth was willing to give up everything she knew. The two women walked all the way to Bethlehem together.

Hear: What did Naomi hear in Ruth's words that made her sure that Ruth wouldn't change her mind?

See: Ruth had never been away from Moab. What do you think she saw on the way to Bethlehem? How do you think she felt when they got to Bethlehem?

Act: When people move to your school, church, or neighborhood, how can you help them feel at home?

Ruth and Naomi's New Life in Bethlehem

Based on Ruth 1:19b–21; 2:1–23

Life in a new place has many surprises. It certainly did for Ruth and Naomi.

"Is this Naomi?" the women in Bethlehem asked. They hadn't seen her for a long, long time.

"Don't call me Naomi," she said. "Call me Mara because I am sad. I have lost my husband and my sons."

Naomi and Ruth the Moabite got to Bethlehem in time for the barley harvest.

Naomi knew that Boaz, a rich relative of her husband, lived there. Perhaps he could help the two widows.

"I'll go and gather grain from a barley field," Ruth said to Naomi. The law said that poor people could gather grain left behind after the field workers cut down the grain.

Naomi agreed. Ruth left to gather what grain she could find. By chance, Ruth went to a field belonging to Boaz. When Boaz came to the field, he asked the man in charge, "Who is the young woman over there?"

"She is the Moabite woman who came with Naomi," he said. "She asked to gather grain in the field. She has worked all morning. She rested only for a little bit."

Boaz went to Ruth. "Gather grain only in my field with my young women. You will be safe here. When you get thirsty, get a drink from the jugs my men have filled."

Ruth bowed down to Boaz. "I'm from Moab. Why are you so kind to me?"

"I've heard how kind you have been to Naomi. I know that you left your family and country to come here with her. May God bless you."

"I hope you will always be kind to me," answered Ruth.

Then Boaz invited Ruth to eat lunch with him. Later he told his men to leave extra grain in the field for Ruth to gather.

When she went home to Naomi, Ruth had a lot of grain. Naomi asked, "Where did you gather so much grain? Whose field were you in?"

"A man named Boaz was kind to me," said Ruth.

"God bless him," said Naomi. "Boaz is one of our close relatives. He can help us."

Ruth returned to Boaz's fields every day during the barley and wheat harvests. She and Naomi had enough food to eat.

Hear: How do you think the man in charge of the field heard about Ruth the Moabite?

See: Imagine leaning over and picking up grain all day. What would you see?

Act: Allowing hungry people to gather grain was the way to feed them in Bible times. It's called *gleaning*. How do we help hungry people today? How can you and your family help?

Naomi's New Family

Based on Ruth 4:1–17

Who is in your family? Naomi lost her family when her husband and sons died. Her family became Ruth. But Naomi longed for children in her family.

As time went by, Boaz decided that he wanted to help Naomi and Ruth. The best way to keep them safe was to buy a field belonging to Naomi. Boaz went to the town's gate. Men gathered there to conduct business. On this day, another relative of Elimelech came by. He had the first right to buy Naomi's field.

"Naomi wants to sell her field," Boaz said to this man. "You have the right to buy it first. What do you want to do? If you don't want to buy it, I am second to get that chance."

"Yes, I will buy it," said the man.

"If you buy the field, you also marry Ruth the Moabite," said Boaz.

"Well, then I don't think I can buy Naomi's field. I can't take Ruth as my wife. You can buy the field and marry Ruth," the man said. To seal the deal, Boaz took off one sandal and gave it to the man. That was like shaking hands to agree on something today.

"May God be with you. May all go well with you, Boaz," said the men at the town's gate. "May God bless you and Ruth with many children."

Boaz and Ruth were married. Ruth had a baby boy. Naomi took care of the baby. She named him Obed. When Obed grew up, he became the father of Jesse and the grandfather of David.

Hear: What do you think the women in Bethlehem said when they heard that Naomi had a grandson?

See: Imagine Naomi holding baby Obed. What might she sing or say to him?

Act: Do any of your friends have babies in their families? What could you do to welcome the baby? If you like, you can write a letter to a baby recently baptized or dedicated at your church.

Queen Vashti Says "No!"

Based on Esther 1:1–22

What do you think it would be like to be a king or queen? Could you do whatever you wanted? Eat dessert first? Stay up late? Queen Vashti decided there was something she would not do.

King Ahasuerus ruled over the land from Ethiopia to India. He liked to have parties to show how rich and important he was. One time he had a party for all the generals and governors of the lands around him. This party lasted for 180 nights.

But one party wasn't enough. When it was over, he had another party. To this one he invited the men of Susa, where his royal palace was. The party was in the beautiful courtyard. The marble pillars were draped with expensive blue cloth held up by silver rings. The floor glimmered with beautiful colored stones.

At the same time, Queen Vashti gave a party for the women of Susa. They were in another part of the palace, where the women of the court lived.

On the seventh night of this party, the king was feeling pretty good. He wanted to show off his beautiful queen. He sent seven servants to get Queen Vashti.

"The king says you are to come to him. And wear your crown. He wants all the men to see what a beautiful queen he has."

Vashti knew it was dangerous not to obey the king. But she was having her own party. She gave the servants a message for the king: "I will not come."

When the king got Queen Vashti's message, he was angry. He said to his advisors, "This cannot be! No one can refuse the king's command! What can I do?"

The advisors huddled and talked. They said to King Ahasuerus, "The queen cannot be allowed to do this. If our wives find out that the queen did not obey the king, they will stop listening to us. You must remove the crown from Vashti. Send word to all the people of your kingdom that she is no longer your queen."

That is what the king did. Meanwhile, Vashti never had to come to the king again.

Hear: Pretend you are in the huddle with the king's advisors. What are they saying?

See: If you were going to build a model of the palace courtyard, what would you use for the marble pillars or the floor with beautiful stones?

Act: Vashti was a strong woman when she refused to do what the king wanted. What strong women do you know or know about?

Esther, a New Queen

Based on Esther 2:1–4, 7–12, 16–18

Have you ever done something when you were angry and later you were sorry you did it? Maybe you threw a toy when it didn't work right? Or perhaps you tore up a picture you were drawing? Later you wanted to play with the toy, or you wanted to work on the picture some more. Too late. King Ahasuerus had a similar problem.

King Ahasuerus finally calmed down after he took the crown from Vashti. But now he wanted a queen, and he didn't have one. Some young men servants suggested a plan. "Why don't you gather at the palace all the beautiful young women who aren't married? Put them in the care of Hegai, who is in charge of the women's quarters. He can get them ready so that you can choose one to be queen in place of Vashti."

The king liked the idea. So some of his servants went throughout the realm to

find beautiful young women. One of these women was Esther. Her mother and father had died. Her cousin Mordecai took care of her. He said, "Esther, don't tell anyone at the palace that you are a Jew."

Hegai liked Esther right away. He believed that she was beautiful and also kind. He made sure that she had the best of everything, from beauty treatments to food. Every day Mordecai walked back and forth in front of the women's quarters so that he could see how Esther was doing.

After one year, the beautiful young women were to go before King Ahasuerus. The women went in to the king, one at a time. When the king saw Esther, she won his love immediately. The king placed the queen's crown on Esther's head. Then he had a huge feast in her honor and declared a holiday. Long live Queen Esther!

Hear: What do you think the king said when he saw Esther? What do you think Mordecai said when he heard that Esther was the new queen?

See: Who do you think came to the feast in honor of Queen Esther? How do you think the tables looked loaded with food?

Act: Esther had a lot to do to get ready to be queen. When have you had to get ready to do something new? What did you do?

Hooray for Queen Esther!

Based on Selections from Esther 3; 4; 6; 8; 9

Vashti was brave to refuse the king. Now Esther has her chance to be brave.

Haman was the highest official in the king's court. A law said that everyone had to bow down to him. Mordecai, Esther's cousin, would not do that. He bowed down only to God. Haman was furious. He got King Ahasuerus to let him write a law that anyone who didn't bow down to Haman would die.

When Mordecai heard about this law, he tore his clothes and cried. He knew that he and all Jews were in big trouble.

Mordecai sent word to Esther that she had to help her people. But Esther said, "I have not been called to come to the king for thirty days. If you go to the king when he hasn't called for you, you will die."

Mordecai sent Esther another message. "Esther, don't think that you are safe because you are the queen. Maybe you are in the palace just so that you can save your people. Now is the time to be brave."

Esther had a plan. She invited the king and Mordecai to dinner. But she didn't say anything to the king about the new law. That night, the king couldn't sleep. A servant read from a book about a time when Mordecai saved the king's life. The king asked, "What has been done for Mordecai?" When he heard that nothing was done for him, the king decided it was time to honor Mordecai.

The king asked Haman, "What should I do to honor a faithful person?"

Haman thought that the king was going to honor him. He said, "Dress him in a royal robe. Have him ride through Susa on your horse."

The king ordered that this be done for Mordecai. Haman knew that he was in big trouble now. When the two men came for dinner the second night, the king asked, "What can I do for you, Esther?"

Esther said, "Please, save my life and the lives of my people."

The king didn't understand. Esther explained about the new law that Haman wrote. Now the

king was angry, but he couldn't take away the law. Instead, he told Esther that her people could protect themselves. They did, but Haman died.

From that time until today, Jews celebrate this story of brave Queen Esther with drama, special food, and games on Purim, in the late winter or early spring.

Hear: What might Esther have said to herself to get enough courage to go to the king?

See: How do you think Mordecai and all the Jews looked when they heard Haman's new law?

Act: What can you and your family do to help people who live in terrible conditions today?

Deborah, a Wise Prophet

Based on Judges 4:1–16; 5:3, 31

Have you ever had a hard time trying to decide what to do? Did you ask someone to help you? This is a story about a woman named Deborah. She helped people make hard decisions.

When the Israelites asked for God's help, God always sent a person to help them. One time, God sent a woman named Deborah who was a great prophet. A prophet is someone who tells people about God and what God wants them to do.

Deborah was a kind and wise leader. Everyone respected and loved her. Deborah sat under her palm tree and helped people make hard decisions. People came from all over to talk to her and listen to what God said to her.

In the land of Hazor, there was a man named Sisera. He was in charge of the army of King Jabin. King Jabin wanted to rule over God's people, the Israelites. So he sent Sisera and the army to capture them.

Around the same time, God spoke to Deborah, "Tell Barak that I want him to take his army and defend my people."

Barak was in charge of the Israelite army. Deborah and Barak were good friends. She told Barak what God told her. Barak trusted Deborah.

He asked her, "Deborah, will you go into battle with me? This is a hard decision, but together we can defend God's people." Deborah agreed to go with him into battle.

Barak gathered ten thousand soldiers. With them, Deborah and Barak defeated Sisera's army.

To thank God, Deborah's son, Abinoam, sang a song in her honor praising God. Today, we call that song "Deborah's Song." After that, the Israelites lived in peace for forty years.

Hear: God spoke to Deborah often. What does it sound like when God talks to you?

See: Who is a wise woman in today's world? Why do you think she is wise?

Act: Deborah helped people when they came to her with hard decisions. How would you help someone making a hard decision?

Hannah's Prayer to God

Based on 1 Samuel 1:1–28

Have you ever wanted something that you didn't have? Was it something small or big?

I wanted something really big! My name is Hannah. I live with my husband, Elkanah. I love my husband, but he doesn't know how sad I am. I cry a lot. I'm not hungry at all. It feels like there is a big hole in my heart. One thing can make it better: a baby.

Elkanah thinks if I eat I'll feel better. He says, "I love you, Hannah. I love you more than ten sons could love you." But it doesn't help. I want a son.

In our world, men can have more than one wife. That might sound weird to you! Elkanah's second wife, Peninnah, lives with us. I'm even sadder when I see how happy she is with her children. It's not easy living together in our village. People don't look at me the same as they do Peninnah. She has children. I don't.

When we go to Shiloh to give sacrifices to God, Elkanah gives more of the sacrifice to Peninnah because she has many children. I get one share to give to God.

I'm also tired of Peninnah making fun of me because I don't have a child. So I decided to do something about it. When we were in Shiloh, I went to the holy place to pray to God. I started to cry, so I prayed with my heart. My lips moved silently. "Please, God, do you see how sad I am because I don't have a son? Remember me. If you give me a son, I promise that he will serve you all his life."

Eli, the priest, was sitting at the door. He had seen me crying and praying by moving my lips. He thought that maybe I was drunk. He stopped me and said, "Don't act like this."

I told him why I was sad and what I had prayed. He listened and blessed me. "Leave here in peace. I pray that God will answer your prayer."

I felt better. Later that year, I had a baby boy. I named him Samuel, which means "God has heard." I remembered my promise to God. When Samuel was older, I took him to Eli so that he could serve God. God heard my prayer, and I will always remember that.

Hear: Imagine that Elkanah is trying to comfort Hannah. What does he say?

See: How do you think Hannah looked after she talked with Eli? How do you think she stood and walked?

Act: What do you want to pray to God for?

Brave Rahab

Based on Joshua 2:1–24

Have you ever wondered if you could do something hard that you had never done before? This story is about a woman named Rahab who did a very brave thing.

Rahab was a Canaanite woman. She lived in a house in the city wall of Jericho. Rahab was both smart and very brave.

One day, Joshua, the leader of God's people the Israelites, sent two men to spy on Jericho. When the spies got to the city wall, they went into Rahab's house.

"Hide us," they said to Rahab. Rahab had heard how God had helped the Israelites. She knew God was with them. She hid the spies under the reeds on her roof.

Meanwhile, the king of Jericho was told that two men from Israel were seen going into Rahab's house. The king sent this message to Rahab: "Send the men who have come to spy on us out so that I can capture them."

"They have already left the city. If you hurry, you can catch them," Rahab said. She sent the king's people away from the spies hiding in her house. Then Rahab went to the roof. She said to the men there, "Come out. I sent the king's people away. I have saved you because I know that your God is with you. Now promise me that you will make sure that my family and I will be safe."

The spies promised Rahab that if she didn't tell anyone about what they were going to do, she and her family would be safe. So Rahab tied a rope to her window so that the spies could climb down the outside of the wall. She told them, "Go toward the hills so that the king's people won't find you. Hide there for three days. Then you can leave."

The spies from Israel gave Rahab a red cord. They said, "Hang this red cord from your window. Bring all your family members to this house. When we return to fight the army of Jericho, we will not harm whoever is with you."

When the spies left, Rahab hung the red cord in the window. Because Rahab was brave and believed that God was with Israel, she saved her entire family. Joshua, the leader of God's people, let them live in the Israelite camp.

Hear: What do you think it sounded like when Rahab hid the spies under her roof?

See: If you could draw a picture of this story, what would you put in it?

Act: Rahab was very brave. Tell a story about a time when you were brave.

Nabal, Abigail, and David

Based on 1 Samuel 25:2–42

When you know two friends are angry with each other, have you tried to tell one of them not to be mad? Abigail convinced David not to stay mad at her husband Nabal.

Before David was king, he traveled with six hundred men. One time, they camped near shepherds who worked for a rich man in Carmel. He owned three thousand sheep and one thousand goats. David sent ten servants to Nabal with a message: "Peace to you. My men and I stayed near your shepherds. We didn't harm them. We didn't take anything from them. Please give my servants all the food you have."

Nabal said, "Who is David? I won't give him anything!"

David's servants told him what happened. David was angry. He told his men, "Put on your swords and get ready to fight!"

Nabal's servant said to Abigail, "David asked your husband for food. Nabal refused. David and his men were good to us when we watched the sheep. They kept us safe. They didn't take anything from us. Your husband is a terrible man. Think about what you can do."

Abigail packed two hundred loaves of bread, one hundred raisin cakes, and two hundred fig cakes, along with grain, lamb to cook, and wine. She got on her donkey and left to find David. She did not tell her husband.

Abigail met David and his soldiers on the hillside. He was still angry. Abigail got off her donkey. She bowed to the ground at David's feet.

"My master," she said, "blame me. Please give this food to your men. Don't get back at Nabal. He is a fool, just as his name says. Don't do something you'll be sorry about. When God makes you king, remember me, your servant."

David looked at the beautiful and wise Abigail. "Bless God who sent you to me," he said. "If you hadn't come, I would have made a great mistake. I will take all that you bring. Go home in peace."

The next morning Abigail told Nabal what she had done. He fainted. Ten days later, he died. When David heard this, he said, "God has gotten back at Nabal. I didn't have to do anything."

Then he sent a servant to Abigail with this message: "Return with my servant and be my wife." She did.

Hear: What did Abigail say to David that helped him make the right decision about Nabal?

See: How many donkeys do you think Abigail needed to take all that food to David?

Act: Abigail was wise and understood people. When have you done something that was wise or showed that you understood how someone felt?

Wise Woman of Tekoa

Based on 2 Samuel 14:1–21

Choosing to love someone when they do something wrong is hard to do. Choosing to love someone when they hurt another person is hard to do. In the Bible, this kind of love is called *mercy*. This is a story about a time King David chose mercy, with the help of a wise woman. Hear her tell the story:

"We had a king named David. King David was heartbroken because his sons were mean. They used their power to hurt each other. They hated one another. One terrible day, one of the king's sons used his power to badly hurt his sister. This made his brother really mad. He was so angry that he killed his brother. Then he ran away from home.

"Now King David had to decide what to do. His daughter was hurt. One of his

sons was dead. The other son was hiding far away. King David was both angry and sad. He didn't know what to do. This was serious business.

"When I heard about the king's troubles, I decided to leave my home in Tekoa to go see him. The people in Tekoa call me wise because I try to help people when they are angry, confused, or scared. I try to use my wisdom to help people in trouble. Joab, David's advisor, knew about the king's troubles and asked me to help. I told King David this story that I hoped would help him decide what to do:

"'I have two sons. They could not stop fighting until one killed his brother. Now I am so sad. My whole family is angry and wants to punish my son who lives. They want to kill him, too! But my husband is dead and so is my other son. If we kill this son, I will be alone. If we kill my son, when will the killing stop?'

"King David wanted to help me. He said, 'I promise, you have my protection and so does your son. I won't let anyone hurt him; I won't even let them touch a hair on his head.'

"Then I asked the king, 'Then what about your son? Will you do the same to protect him?'

"King David blinked his eyes with surprise. His heart grew soft. 'You are right, wise woman. I can love and protect my son, even when he does a terrible thing. I will bring him home.'"

Hear: Do you think King David could still love his son? How did the wise woman help him?

See: Have you ever seen someone hurt someone else? How did it make you feel?

Act: Who is the wisest person you know? What might you ask them?

I Used All My Courage

Based on 2 Samuel 17:17–21

Do you ever think that you are too small or too young to do something important? The girl who tells this story helped a king:

"When I was a little girl, I lived with my family, and David was our king. My father would say, 'King David is not perfect, but he is our king.'

"My mother would often reply, 'He has hard choices to make, but he always trusts God.'

"After King David brought his son Absalom home, his son decided that he wanted to be king. Absalom began gathering support from communities all around the country. He traveled to my town and set up camp here. In my neighborhood, some people loved King David. Others wanted Absalom to be the king. Our town was divided.

"King David sent two of his men to follow Absalom and find out what he planned to do. He still loved his son, but he knew he couldn't trust him.

"There I was, a young girl who wanted to help her king. I followed the men to their hiding place on the edge of town. I told King David's men, 'I can move around my neighborhood and keep an eye on the king's son and all his men. I can come and tell you everything I see. No one will pay attention to me because I belong here.'

"The men agreed. I used all my courage to go back and forth each day to report. One day, a boy whose family supported the king's son saw me talking to the king's men. He ran to tell on me.

"My heart beat fast as I ran with King David's men to my house. My father helped them climb into our well!

"My mother was clever. She covered the well with her towel and piled grain on top. Men who worked for the king's son came around the corner just as she finished. They searched our home. I was afraid, but my mother was brave. She shouted, 'The men you are looking for are not here!'

"The men gave up and ran away. They went across the water in search of King David's men. My

mother lifted the covering from the well. The king's men climbed out and ran in the other direction. They hurried to tell King David all that had happened. I was proud of my family for being brave. But I hated the way our neighborhood was divided."

Hear: Why was the young girl's neighborhood divided?

See: What would you do if you saw that someone was in danger?

Act: How can remembering the story of this brave girl help you when you need to do something hard?

The Widow of Zarephath

Based on 1 Kings 17:8–24

Surprises can be great! Like waking up on your birthday and knowing someone is baking a cake, but you don't know what kind. Listen for surprises in this woman's story:

"I live in the town of Zarephath near Sidon. They call me the Widow of Zarephath because my husband died. I live with my son. We don't have money to buy food. Even if we did, it hasn't rained in so long, there's no food to buy. I knew we would not be able to live much longer.

"I went to get water from the well. A man saw me and said, 'I'm so thirsty, please put some water in my cup. And I'm hungry. Can you give me some bread?' This man was Elijah. He had come from Israel.

"I went to get water for him, but I had to tell the truth, 'I don't have any food for you. At home I have just enough flour and oil to make a loaf of bread for my

son and me. I'm looking for some sticks to make a fire and bake it. It will be our last meal because there's no more food.'

"Elijah told me something that was hard to believe. He said, 'You don't know me, but don't be afraid, just listen. Go home and make the bread. But first make a small loaf for me. The God of Israel says that you will have enough flour and oil to bake bread until it rains again.'

"Really? But I went home and did what he said. What do you think happened? I baked bread each day for my son and me and Elijah. There was always enough flour and oil. It was just like Elijah's God promised.

"Then something terrible happened. My son stopped breathing. How could I help him? I asked Elijah why this was happening. He didn't know. But he did something really amazing.

"Elijah laid my son on his bed. I heard him praying to his God. Then he stretched his hands over my son three times and prayed for him to live. God listened to Elijah. My son started breathing.

"That's when I knew that Elijah was God's prophet. That's when I knew that God's voice was heard by Elijah."

Hear: Who was surprised in this story?

See: Think about how you might tell this story with pictures. Tear pieces of colored paper and make a collage.

Act: Bake bread using flour, oil, and herbs. Make two loaves, one to eat at home and one to share with someone. Tell them the story of the Widow of Zarephath.

The Hardest Thing

Based on Genesis 22:1–19

Some stories, even some stories in the Bible, make it really easy to tell who the "good" people are. The "good" people are really good. In this story, Abraham is the really good person. He is so good that he trusts God even when God asks him to do the hardest thing. This story can be hard to read because God asks Abraham to do such a hard, scary thing. And it doesn't tell us what Abraham is thinking. Remember, this story is about telling everyone how much Abraham trusts God. That's the good news in this very hard story.

Abraham didn't know that God wanted to test him when God called, "Abraham!"

"Here I am," Abraham said.

"Take your son, Isaac, whom you love so much, up a mountain. I will show you which one. There you will do a very hard thing, the hardest thing. You will offer your son as a burnt offering."

People offered gifts to God by burning them in those days. Usually it was an animal like a lamb, not a human like Isaac.

Abraham got up early the next morning and packed for the trip. He took a donkey, firewood, fire, a knife, his son Isaac, and two servants from his house. After traveling for three days, Abraham saw the mountain, still very far away. He left the donkey and the two servants. He said, "We'll be back after we worship God on the mountain. Stay here."

Abraham put the firewood on Isaac's back. Abraham carried the fire and the knife for the sacrifice.

Isaac noticed that they had everything for a burnt offering except the lamb. "Father," he said, "where is the lamb for the burnt offering?"

"God will provide the lamb, my son," Abraham said.

Now comes the scary part.

On the mountain, Abraham piled up the wood for a big fire. He tied up Isaac and put him on the pile. Just as he picked up the knife, a messenger

from God called from heaven, "Abraham! Stop! Don't touch Isaac! Now I know that you trust God. You were willing to do the hardest thing, hurt your son, when God told you to."

Nearby, Abraham saw a ram stuck in a bush. He offered it as a burnt offering instead of Isaac.

God's messenger called to Abraham, "God says, 'Because you have done such a hard thing and were prepared to offer your son to me, I will make you this promise. Your family will be as many as the stars in the sky and sand on the beach. And they will be safe for a long, long time. Everyone in the world will be blessed because of your family.'"

What a great blessing! Abraham and Isaac went back to the servants. They all went home together.

Hear: What's the scariest story you've ever heard? How did it make you feel? Did it make you wonder about God? What did you wonder?

See: Have you ever seen something you needed in an unexpected place, like the ram in the story? What was it?

Act: What sorts of things do you think God asks you to do?

Dreams and Promises

Based on Genesis 28:10–22

Do you dream when you sleep? Dreams are interesting, aren't they? They are like movies in our minds. Some people believe God speaks to us in our dreams. This is the story of one of Jacob's dreams.

Jacob's brother, Esau, was angry, so angry that he wanted to kill his brother. His parents told Jacob to leave Beersheba and go to Haran. Along the way, when the sun went down, Jacob stopped to sleep. He used a stone as a pillow. He lay on the ground and fell asleep.

Jacob dreamed of a staircase that went from the ground up into the sky. Angels, messengers of God, walked up and down on the staircase. They seemed to go back and forth, from earth to heaven and back again.

God stood next to Jacob. God said, "I am the Lord, the God of your father Abraham and of Isaac."

God made many great promises to Jacob. God said, "You know this land, the

place where you just stopped to sleep? I will give it to you and all your family that come after you. Your people will spread across the earth, like sand on the beach. They will spread to the north, south, east, and west. Your family will bless all the families of the earth. You will leave this place, and go to many other places. And I will bring you back here. I will be with you the whole time, until I have kept all my promises."

Then Jacob woke up. "Wow! I just stopped here to sleep. Now I know that this is God's house, and the gate of heaven."

This place and even his stone pillow were now very special to Jacob. So he gave the place a new name, Bethel. He stood the stone up and poured oil on it. This was a way to remember this sacred place.

Then Jacob made a promise to God. "If God keeps God's promises to me— gives me food and clothes and brings me safely back home—then the Lord will be my God. This stone will be God's house. And I will give you, God, a tenth of everything you give to me."

Hear: Have you ever heard a voice in your dreams? What did the voice say?

See: What do you think an angel, a messenger of God, looks like?

Act: Jacob made a promise to God. What might you promise to God?

Moses and the Special Holy Place

Based on Exodus 3:1–12

Is there a place that is special to you? A place you like to be? Moses finds himself in a special place in this story.

Taking care of his new family's flock was a big change for Moses. He never had to do that when he lived in Pharaoh's house in Egypt. On this day, he took the flock far from home to the sunny side of the mountain.

Moses saw a bush burning bright. But the bush wasn't burning up. Moses said, "I've got to see this up close! Why isn't that bush burning up?"

God saw Moses heading to the bush. God called, "Moses, Moses."

"Here I am," said Moses.

"Stay back," said God. "Take off your shoes. You are standing on special holy ground." Then God said, "Your family has known me a long time; going way back to Abraham, Isaac, and Jacob."

All of this scared Moses. He hid his face.

God said more, "I see my people in Egypt are having a hard time. I hear them crying out because their masters make them work too hard. I know that they are hurting. So I'm here to rescue them from the Egyptians. I want to take them from Egypt to a new place to live, a land of milk and honey. Other people already live there, but I have heard my people cry. I've seen how badly and unfairly the Egyptians treat them. Moses, I want you to rescue my people from Pharaoh."

Moses said, "I can't rescue your people. Pharaoh won't listen to me at all."

"You can, because I'll be with you," said God. "When it's all over, come back here to this special holy place and worship me."

Hear: What sounds do you think Moses heard when the bush was burning?

See: Have you ever seen something you couldn't explain with words? What was it? What did you think about it?

Act: In the story, God tells Moses that God is with people who are hurting or treated unfairly. What are some ways you can help others know that about God?

Terrible, Awful Times

Exodus 5–11; 12:21–23, 29–36

African Americans tell this Bible story because they were once slaves. Jews tell this story every year at Passover. This story reminds us how God is always with us, even in terrible, awful times.

God gave Moses and his brother, Aaron, a message for Pharaoh: "Let my people go into the wilderness to worship God together for a few days."

"Which god are you talking about?" asked Pharoah. "Get back to work!"

"God! Help your people with these terrible, awful times!" shouted Moses.

"Just wait," said God. "See the power I have. Remind my people of the promises I made to them long ago. I will lead them to a new place to live. Say and do what I tell you. Pharaoh will let you go."

Each time Pharaoh said no, God did some terrible, awful thing. First, God turned Moses' walking stick into a snake! Then God turned the water in Egypt into blood! Frogs, mosquitos, and flies got into the food. The Egyptians and their animals got sick and the animals died. Thunder, hail, and hungry locusts destroyed the crops. Everything was completely dark for three days!

So many terrible, awful things happened, but only to the Egyptians. But none of these terrible, awful things from God changed Pharaoh's mind.

God had one more terrible, awful thing planned. Moses told his people to mark their doors with lamb's blood so that God would know where they lived. At midnight, God made the oldest child in each Egyptian family die. Pharaoh woke to the cries of the Egyptian parents.

"Moses and Aaron," called Pharaoh, "I'll do what you asked. Worship your God. Also, bless me so that these terrible, awful things stop!"

God's people left quickly for the land that God had promised them.

Hear: Where do you hear stories told over and over? Why are they told so often?

See: Have you ever seen a leader act in an unfair way, unfair like Pharaoh?

Act: When you see leaders act unfairly, what can you do to change their minds? How can God help you like God helped Moses?

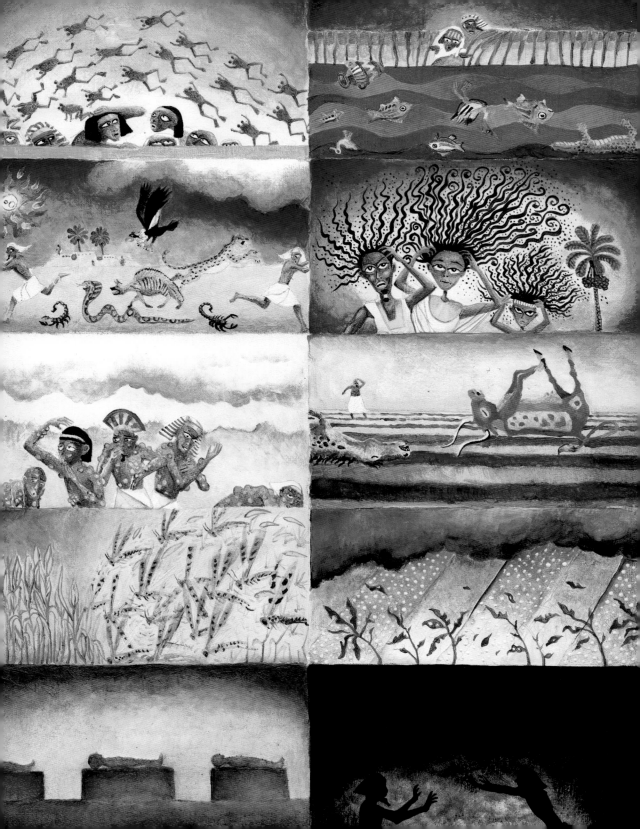

Walking on Dry Land

Exodus 14:5–31

Have you ever felt completely free? Like when summer vacation begins? Then what if someone gave you chores to do? That would be the worst! That's what happens in this story. Right when the Israelites think they are free, Pharaoh sends his army after them.

Remember the previous story and all the terrible, awful things that happened to the Egyptians? God wanted Pharaoh to let the Israelites go, and he did.

But after they were gone, he thought, *"What am I doing? Who will make my bricks? I need the Israelites back. Quick!"* Pharaoh called for his fastest chariots so that he could chase after the people he had just let go.

The Israelites saw them coming, and they were scared. They shouted to God.

"We told you something bad would happen. We should have stayed and worked for the Egyptians. Now we'll be killed by this army in the middle of nowhere!"

"Don't be afraid!" said Moses. "God will protect us. You'll never have to see the Egyptians again."

God heard this and said, "Why are you so worried? Tell everyone to keep moving to the sea. Moses, you will part the waters so that my people will walk on dry land."

God's messenger and a tall cloud that was leading the Israelites moved behind them to protect them from the Egyptians. Moses stretched his arm over the sea. God blew the water out of the way so that the people could walk across on dry land. The Egyptians followed them. God lit the tall cloud with fire. The Egyptian army was frightened. Their chariot wheels stopped turning, and they tried to run away. God told Moses to stretch his arm over the water again. The water crashed back on the dry land. The army drowned in the sea right in front of the Israelites.

They realized what God had done for them. They believed that God was their God, and finally they trusted Moses.

Hear: How does the wind sound when it blows across the water?

See: Have you ever seen the ocean or a big lake? What it would look like if God blew the water out of the way?

Act: Moses was a brave leader. How can you be a brave leader?

Just Enough

Exodus 16:1–31

Have you ever felt really grumpy? Or grumpy and tired? Or grumpy, tired, and hungry all at the same time? If you have, then you know what it was like for the Israelites after they left Egypt.

It had been two months since the Israelites left Egypt. That's a long time on your own in the desert. They complained to Moses and Aaron, "We were slaves in Egypt, but at least we had enough food to eat."

Now they were so hungry that they thought they might die!

"They know I can hear them when they complain, right?" God asked Moses.

"I'm not sure they do," said Moses.

"Okay. I have a plan. It will help them know that I hear their grumbling, and

I will feed them. But it will test how well they follow my instructions." God told Moses the plan.

"Everybody, listen," said Moses and Aaron. "Why complain to us? God can hear you and has a plan to feed you. When you have meat at night, God wants you to remember. Remember all the terrible, awful things God saved you from in Egypt. When you have bread to eat in the morning, you will see God's greatness. Please, follow God's instructions."

That night quail landed in the Israelites' camp. Now they had meat to eat. In the morning when the dew lifted, flakey stuff was left on the ground.

"What is this stuff?" the Israelites asked. "This is the bread that God has given us," Moses said. "And these are your instructions: Every morning gather just enough of it for your family. Don't save any. You have to trust that there will be more tomorrow."

They gathered the flakey stuff and ate it. Some folks didn't follow the directions and tried to save some for later. It grew worms and got really awful. This made Moses angry. After a few days the people knew they would have more each day. Morning after morning, they gathered just enough.

On the sixth day, God had something special in store for the Israelites. That morning they gathered enough for two days.

"Tomorrow is a day for you to rest. It is called the Sabbath," said Moses. "It is a day for God. Gather enough for two days and cook it today. Tomorrow, don't go out to gather anything."

Some Israelites did try to gather food on the seventh day, but nothing was there. Now they knew that they were to rest on the seventh day. God would give them food.

Hear: What does it sound like when your stomach growls? What do you like to eat when you are so hungry?

See: What do you think the flakey stuff that God gave the Israelites for bread looked like?

Act: What would you do if there were no grocery stores to buy food? What did Moses and God do?

God Is Where the Water Is

Based on Exodus 17:1–7

What do you do when you are thirsty? When you are really thirsty after playing on a hot day? The Israelites were really thirsty. But they had nowhere to get water.

So many Israelites left Egypt that they could travel only a short way each day. One day they stopped in a place that had no water to drink. No water fountains. Nowhere to buy bottles of water. Not even a swimming pool or a lake. The people were very thirsty. People can't live very long without water. They were afraid they would die!

The people had complained to Moses before this day. Now, because they were so thirsty and scared, they were really mean to Moses.

"Give us water to drink right now!" they shouted.

"Why are you being mean to me?" Moses asked. "Why are you testing God?"

The Israelites were so thirsty. They had forgotten when God saved them from the terrible, awful work Pharaoh forced them to do in Egypt.

"Why did you even bother making us leave Egypt? Was it to have us all get so thirsty and die here in the middle of nowhere?" they asked.

The Israelites were really scared and angry this time. Moses knew it was time to talk with God.

"What am I going to do with these people, God? They're about to throw rocks at me!"

God answered with a plan for Moses to get water for the people. "Take some leaders and the same walking stick you used to turn the Nile River into blood in Egypt. Go away from the people. I will be standing on a rock. Hit that rock with your walking stick. Watch water—enough for everyone—come out of it."

Moses did all that God said. The leaders saw it happen. The people remembered that place. They called it Massah and Meribah because they were mean to Moses and tested God there. But God was with them anyway.

Hear: What does your voice sound like when you are very scared?

See: Have you ever seen water coming out of a spring? That's when water seeps up through the ground. Kind of like coming from a rock!

Act: Have you ever noticed how heavy water is? Ask a grown-up to help you lift a gallon of water. Lots of people in the world don't have water faucets in their house. They have to carry water for cooking and washing a long way. Can you imagine having to carry all the water for your bath? How many buckets do you think it would take?

Joshua Leads with God's Help

Based on Joshua 1:1–17

What do you think happens when a great leader dies? Moses was a great leader of God's people. Moses, with God's help, led the people out of slavery in Egypt. But God told Moses he would die before reaching the Promised Land.

Moses grew old and died. Now who would lead the people into the Promised Land? God and Moses had already prepared Joshua to lead. And Joshua had everything he needed to do a good job.

First, Joshua had God. God talked to Joshua all the time. God told Joshua, "Moses is dead. Get ready to lead the people across the Jordan River."

God promised to give them the land between the Mediterranean Sea and the Euphrates River. God promised!

God also said, "Be strong and brave! Do not be afraid. I am with you wherever you go." God repeated these words to Joshua many times.

Second, Joshua had instructions. God told Joshua, "Remember the instructions

Moses wrote down for you. Think about them. Say them out loud. Be brave, and obey those instructions! If the people obey all of Moses' instructions, they will succeed."

Third, Joshua had helpers. Joshua told his helpers, "Walk around and tell the people to get ready. God promised us the land on the other side of the Jordan River. Three days from today, we will cross the Jordan to take this land!"

Joshua and his helpers talked to the people. They told them exactly what to do to go to their new land.

And the people agreed to follow and obey Joshua. They said to him, "We will obey you. We will go where you tell us to go."

Joshua was the new leader of the people of Israel.

Hear: What words did Joshua hear that helped him believe he could lead the people? What words help you believe you can do good things?

See: How do you think the people looked when they heard that Moses had died? Why? How do you think they looked by the end of the story? Why?

Act: Following Moses' instructions was an important part of the story. These instructions were from God. What instructions from God do you follow?

March, Make Music, and Shout

Based on Joshua 6:1–21

In the time of the stories of Jacob and Joshua, cities had strong walls of stone around them. The walls kept enemies and wild animals out. At night the gates were locked. This story is about God giving the Israelites a city called Jericho. You will find out what happens to the walls around Jericho.

When Joshua and the Israelites were near Jericho, the city gates were locked tightly. No one could come in or out of the city.

"Look," said God to Joshua, "I have given Jericho, its king, and army to you. This is how you will take the city. Have your soldiers march around the city walls one time. Do this every day for six days. Have seven priests with trumpets walk in front of God's special chest that holds the Ten Commandments. On the seventh day, march around the city seven times. The priests should blow the trumpets.

After the seventh time, tell the priests to blow one long, loud blast. Tell the Israelites to shout as loudly as they can when they hear this trumpet blast! Then stand back, because those great big walls around Jericho will fall down. Then the people can walk straight into the city!"

That's all they had to do: March, make music, and shout, and the walls were to fall! Joshua gave the instructions. Everyone listened carefully. The soldiers marched around the city one time each day for six days. On the seventh day, they marched around the city seven times, and the priests blew the trumpets. On the seventh time, the priests blew one long blast on the trumpets.

Joshua yelled, "Shout, because God has given you Jericho!" When the people shouted, the walls of Jericho fell down. Crash! Boom! Crash!

But before the people went into Jericho, Joshua said, "Destroy everything in the city in honor of God. But protect Rahab and her family, because she protected our spies. Destroy everything else. Do not take anything from the city. All the silver, gold, bronze, and iron are for God. If you take them, Israel will be punished. It will be your fault."

The people walked into Jericho and destroyed everything. But they did not harm Rahab and her family. They took them to live in their camp.

Hear: Listen to the sounds in this story. The sounds of people marching, trumpets blowing. The sounds of shouting and walls falling. What a noise that must have been!

See: How do you think the Israelites felt when they saw the big wall around the city of Jericho?

Act: The Israelites might have left when they saw the walls around Jericho. But they followed God's directions and won the city. When have you thought something was too hard to do? Who helped you?

Remember, Choose, Serve

Based on Joshua 24:1–24

Look around you. What good things has God given you? Home? Family? Pets? When you stop to think about how good God is to you, you remember to be good to others in return. The Israelites had to be reminded of that in this story.

Joshua called all the leaders of Israel to a place called Shechem.

"God told me to tell you this," Joshua said. "'A long time ago, your ancestors served other gods. I brought Abraham to Canaan and gave him a son, Isaac. I gave Isaac two sons, Jacob and Esau. I gave Esau a mountain, Mount Seir. I sent Jacob and his family to Egypt for food. Your ancestors were slaves in Egypt. So I sent Moses and Aaron to help them get out. It was not easy for Pharaoh to let you go.

'When your ancestors left Egypt, I helped them cross the Reed Sea. After that, they lived in the desert for a long time. I led them to many places, including Jericho. In each place, they had to fight so many people. And I made sure they won every fight!'"

Joshua had more to say from God, "'I, God, gave you land, cities, and houses for free! You didn't even plant the gardens that give you fruit and olives. I gave all of that to you. I made sure you ate good food!'"

Then Joshua added, "God did all of this for you. Now respect God. Worship and serve our God and no other gods. Today you have a choice to make. You can choose to serve other gods or you can serve the God who has done all this for you. My family and I are going to serve God."

The people said, "God rescued us from slavery in Egypt. God has always made sure we were safe. Yes, we will serve God!"

"Remember," warned Joshua, "God does not like it when people serve other gods. Our God is holy. If you try to serve our God and other gods at the same time, you will be in big trouble. Our God will not be happy."

"No, no!" shouted the people. "We will serve God, the God who has been with us all along!"

Choose today whom you will serve.

"Then that is your choice. Remember, you chose to worship and serve God."
The people said, "Yes, we have! We will worship and serve our God!"

Hear: What did you learn about God from Joshua's speech to the people?

See: Look around you again and think about your family. How has God been with you? Ask family members this question too.

Act: How can you and your family worship and serve God today?

Samuel Tells a Hard Truth

Based on 1 Samuel 2:18–3:20

Have you ever had to tell someone bad news? Were you nervous? How did you tell them? Samuel has bad news to tell the priest Eli.

Samuel, a young boy, lived in God's temple. He helped Eli the priest. Every year Samuel's parents, Hannah and Elkanah, came to visit him. Each year his mother made a new robe to bring to Samuel. Samuel loved God. Eli loved God, too. But Eli's sons didn't follow God's ways. They did terrible things. Although Eli loved his sons, God was angry about the things they did.

In those days, the priest's sons became priests too. But because they were so bad, Eli's sons couldn't become priests. Someone had to tell Eli. That someone was Samuel, the boy who helped Eli.

One night, while Samuel and Eli were asleep, Samuel heard someone call, "Samuel!"

Samuel thought it was Eli. He got up and hurried to Eli. Samuel said, "Here I am!"

Eli said, "I didn't call you. Go back to sleep."

Then it happened again. "Samuel. Samuel." Samuel ran to Eli.

"Here I am!"

Again Eli said, "I didn't call you. Go back to sleep."

A third time, Samuel heard his name, and he went to Eli. "I'm here," he said. "You called me."

This time Eli knew that God had called Samuel. But Samuel had never heard God call him, so he didn't know.

"Samuel," said Eli, "listen for your name again. When you hear it, say, 'Yes, I am listening.'"

When Samuel heard his name again, he said, "Yes, I am listening!"

Then God gave Samuel this hard message for Eli. "Samuel, I am getting ready to do something that will make people's ears tingle! Eli's sons are bad. They do terrible things. They have disobeyed me. I am going to punish them. They will not be priests like their father."

In the morning Eli asked Samuel what God had said.

Samuel told Eli the bad news about his sons.

Eli said, "God is God. God makes the right decisions."

Hear: Samuel did not know what God's voice sounded like. What do you think God's voice sounds like?

See: How do you think Eli looked when Samuel told him what God had said?

Act: Eli's sons didn't follow in the ways God wanted them to. When you listen for God's voice, what do you think God wants you to do for others? For God's world?

Samuel Finds a New King

Based on 1 Samuel 8:1–22; 9:1–27; 10:1

Have you ever tried to warn someone that something they were doing wasn't a good idea? Or have you ever tried to do the right thing, and your friends just wanted to do the wrong thing? When this happened to Samuel, he talked with God.

Samuel, that young boy who worked with the priest Eli, was very old now. He had spent his life serving God. His grown-up sons were judges. But they weren't good judges. Just like Eli's sons, they didn't follow God's ways.

The Israelites were fed up with Samuel's sons. They came to Samuel. "We want a king," they said, "not a judge like one of your sons. Find us a king to be our judge and rule over us! That's what we want."

Samuel didn't think that this was a good idea. As he always did when he had a problem, Samuel talked to God.

"What should I do?" Samuel asked. "A king won't help them!"

"Samuel," God said, "just give them a king. Don't fight with them. They don't follow my ways anyway. But you must tell them everything that a king will do to them."

This upset Samuel. He knew that if the people followed God, they would not want a king.

Samuel called the people together. He said, "If you want a king, that's fine. But I want you to know what it will be like to have a king rule over you. A king won't treat you fairly. A king will take all your land from you. A king will make you work hard, and you won't like it. Everything you have will belong to the king, not you. And when you ask God to help you, God won't help you because you wanted a king instead of God."

But the people didn't care. They wanted to be just like everyone else and have a king they could see. They didn't care if God helped them or not. Samuel knew this was a bad idea, but he agreed to find a king.

With God's help, Samuel found Saul. Samuel poured oil over Saul's head. He said, "God makes you the king of God's people, Israel."

Hear: The people were angry that Samuel's sons were not fair to them. What do you say when someone isn't being fair to you?

See: Try standing like you think the people stood when they came to Samuel to demand a king. Why did they want a king?

Act: What can you do to stand up for yourself when you are treated unfairly? Who can help you?

A Brand-New King

Based on 1 Samuel 16:1–13

Can you tell if someone is friendly by looking at them? Sometimes you can and sometimes you can't. Usually it takes more time to get to know a person. Samuel got help from God when he was looking for a new king.

Samuel sat quietly with a sad look on his face. Samuel was sad because God had decided that Saul could no longer be king over God's people. Saul did not have a kind heart.

"Samuel, how much longer will you be sad?" God asked.

Samuel didn't know how to get over being sad. But God said, "Samuel, I want you to go to Bethlehem. My next king is there!"

"God," said Samuel, "you know what a temper Saul has. If he hears that I am looking for a new king, I don't know what he will do."

"Take an animal for a sacrifice with you to Bethlehem. When you get there, invite a man named Jesse and his sons to come with you."

"But how will I know who the next king is?" asked Samuel.

"Don't worry, I'll show you," said God.

Samuel chose an animal for the sacrifice and went to Bethlehem. The people were afraid of Samuel. But Samuel said, "Don't worry, I'm just here to worship God."

When he saw Jesse, he said, "Why don't you and your sons come with me?"

Now Jesse had some good-looking sons. When Samuel saw Eliab, Jesse's oldest son, he thought, *This must be the new king.*

But God told Samuel, "No, not this one. I'll tell you who it is when I see him. I can see people's hearts, and that's what matters to me."

Samuel saw seven of Jesse's sons. Each one looked like a good choice to Samuel. But God just kept saying, "No, not him. I see people's hearts, and that's what matters to me."

Samuel had seen all the sons. God had not chosen any of them. Samuel asked Jesse, "Do you have any more sons?"

Jesse said, "I have one more. My youngest son is out watching the sheep."

"Bring him here," said Samuel.

David came right away. Samuel saw David with his red hair and bright eyes. He heard God's voice say, "That's the one!"

God saw David's heart and knew he was a good person. "He will be the next king of my people!" declared God.

David was still a young man. He didn't know that one day he would be the king of all God's people. Samuel poured oil on David's head. Then God's Spirit came to David and stayed with him for the rest of his life.

Hear: God spoke to Samuel when Samuel was sad. What might God's voice sound like to people who are sad?

See: How do you think David's brothers looked when Samuel poured oil on David's head?

Act: Samuel poured oil on David's head. Dip your fingers in some kitchen oil, such as olive oil. What does it feel like? Imagine it running down your face and over your head.

David Meets Goliath

Based on 1 Samuel 17:1–58

Have you ever been told that you couldn't do something because you weren't big enough? People didn't think David could do much because he was just a young shepherd. But David showed them that you don't have to be a grown-up to do something really big.

When Saul was king over God's people, they were fighting the Philistines. One of the Philistines, Goliath, was as tall as a house. He wore bronze armor all over his body.

Goliath stood in front of Saul's army and yelled at God's people, "Send out someone to fight me!"

Saul and God's people were scared. Goliath was frightening. For forty days, Goliath stood in front of Saul's army, but no one would fight him.

Then, one day, David left his sheep to take food to his brothers. They were in Saul's army. When he got there, he saw Goliath. David asked, "Why won't anyone fight him?"

This made his brothers angry. They thought he just came to watch a battle. "What did I do wrong this time?" David asked. "It was just a question!"

David knew that the soldiers were afraid of Goliath, so he found King Saul. "King Saul, don't worry. I will fight this man!"

But Saul said, "You are just a young man. You cannot fight that big man who is an experienced warrior."

But Saul forgot that shepherds fight lions and bears to keep their sheep safe. David trusted in God, and God kept him safe when he guarded his sheep. He was sure that God would keep him safe now. David picked up five stones for his slingshot.

When David walked out, Goliath laughed. He wanted to fight a man, not a youth. But David knew that he could win because God was with him.

David said, "You come to fight me with sword and spear. But God is with me. I will defeat you!"

David put a stone in his slingshot. He slung it and hit Goliath so hard that he fell flat on his face! Then David picked up Goliath's sword. When the Philistines saw this, they ran away.

Because David knew God was with him, he did a big thing and won the battle for all of God's people.

Hear: Goliath was a very big man with a loud voice. What do you think it sounded like when Goliath yelled at God's people?

See: Which part of this story will you remember? Try making a picture with torn paper, crayons, or markers to show this part of the story.

Act: David was brave because he trusted that God was with him. When can you be brave because you know God will help you?

Taking Special Care

Based on 2 Samuel 6:1–22

Have you ever had something that was special to you? How did you take care of it? This is a story about something special that God wanted David to watch over very carefully.

When David was king, he went to the land called Judah to get God's special chest. It was special because it contained the Ten Commandments that God had given Moses. God's chest lived in Judah. King David said, "It is time the chest came to live with me in Jerusalem."

King David knew that the chest was special to God. David wanted it to be safe. While they were carrying it, the chest started to fall off its cart. Uzzah caught it with his hand. But this upset God. They were not taking good care of the chest.

King David was so upset that he regretted taking the special chest from Judah. So he left it with a man named Obed-edom. He and his family took good care of it for three months. This made God happy.

After King David knew that God was no longer upset, he went to Obed-edom's house. "I think it's time that the chest came home with me to Jerusalem," King David said.

This time, King David made sure that the chest was given special care. He didn't want it to be dropped. He thanked Obed-edom and blessed him.

When King David arrived in Jerusalem with the chest, he danced and celebrated in the streets. He put the chest in the tent that he had set up for it.

King David blessed the people. He gave each family a loaf of bread, a raisin cake, and a date cake so that they could celebrate, too.

Hear: David and the people were happy that the chest came to live in Jerusalem. What do you think the celebration sounded like when it arrived?

See: How do you think David danced when he brought the chest to Jerusalem? Dance like you think David did.

Act: Think of something special to you or your family. How can you celebrate that you have it?

Best Friends

Based on 1 Samuel 20:1–42

Who's your best friend? What are some things you like about your best friend? David and Jonathan were best friends. Listen for how Jonathan helped David when David was in trouble.

David was a loyal worker for King Saul. But Saul was angry with him. Saul was so angry that he wanted to hurt David. However, David was best friends with Jonathan, Saul's son.

"Jonathan," said David, "I think your father, Saul, wants to hurt me. Maybe even kill me."

Jonathan said, "No, that can't be right."

But David insisted that Saul wanted to hurt him.

Jonathan told David, "Whatever you want me to do, I will do."

David said, "Here's the plan. King Saul will hold a special dinner tomorrow night to celebrate the new moon. I'm supposed to sit with him. I won't go, but I'll hide in the field until it's dark. If King Saul misses me, tell him I have gone to Bethlehem. If King Saul becomes angry, you'll know he wants to hurt me."

Jonathan thought this was a good plan. He said, "I'll do this. If my father is angry with you, I'll come and tell you because you are my best friend. I will shoot an arrow near where you are hiding. If I tell my servant, 'Get the arrow. It is on this side of you,' you know it is safe for you to come back. But if I say, 'The arrow is beyond you,' leave, because you are not safe here."

The next night, David went into the field and hid behind a big rock. At the

dinner, Saul didn't ask about David. But the second night after the new moon, King Saul asked Jonathan, "Where is David? He wasn't here for the dinner last night either."

"He went to visit his family in Bethlehem," Jonathan told his father.

When Saul heard this, he became angry. "Why did you let him go? Bring him back to me! I am angry at him!"

The next morning Jonathan went to the field. He shot an arrow near where David was hiding. To his servant, he said, "Isn't the arrow beyond you?"

Jonathan told the servant to go back. Then David and Jonathan kissed and cried. Jonathan said, "Go in peace. We will be friends forever."

David left, and Jonathan went back home.

Hear: Saul became angry when he found out that David was gone. What does it feel like when someone is upset with you?

See: David hid in a big field and waited for Jonathan to return. What do you think David's hiding place looked like?

Act: David and Jonathan were best friends. Who is your best friend? What do you like to do together?

David Keeps a Promise

Based on 2 Samuel 9:1–13

How long do you think you should remember a promise to a friend? A week? A month? A year? David made a promise to his friend Jonathan. He remembered it years later and did what he had promised.

David was king. David and Jonathan were best friends. The last time they were together, David promised to care for any children that Jonathan had. Now King Saul and his son Jonathan were dead.

A servant in the king's palace was brought to King David. "Are you Ziba who worked for King Saul?" asked the king.

"I'm ready to serve you," answered Ziba.

"Tell me. Is there anyone left in Jonathan's family?" King David asked. "I want to keep my promise to Jonathan and take care of his family."

"Yes," said Ziba, "Jonathan's son Mephibosheth, whose feet have been hurt since he was five, is at the house of Machir."

"Bring him to me," said the king.

When Mephibosheth came before King David, he bowed so low that his head touched the ground. "Are you Mephibosheth, the son of Jonathan and the grandson of Saul?" the king asked.

"I'm ready to serve you," said Mephibosheth.

"I promised your father that I would care of his family," said King David. "All the lands that belonged to your grandfather King Saul now belong to you. And you are invited to eat with me and my family here every day."

Mephibosheth bowed down to the king again.

King David called for Ziba. He told him, "Mephibosheth owns all the land that belonged to Saul. You are to take care of them. But Mephibosheth will live here."

"I will do whatever you say, King David," said Ziba.

From that day on, Mephibosheth ate with the king, just like the king's sons. That is how David kept his promise to Jonathan.

Hear: What good news did Mephibosheth hear in this story?

See: How do you think King David looked at Mephibosheth when he came to him?

Act: King David wanted to keep his promise to Jonathan. To do that, he showed love to Mephibosheth, who was disabled. How could you show love to someone who is differently abled?

Giving Up Isn't Really Easy

Based on Job 1–2

Sometimes people think that when something is hard to do, giving up is easy. But it may be that when you give up, you miss out on important things. Have you ever refused to give up on something that was important to you?

Job was a good man. He had lots of children and friends, and he had a lot of things. Job followed God and lived his life in the ways that God wanted.

One day, God said to Satan, an accusing lawyer in heaven, "Don't you see Job, isn't he great? No one is as good or faithful to me as Job is."

"I bet Job wouldn't be faithful to you if he had nothing. He's only happy because he has his family and a lot of money and food," Satan teased.

God said, "Take everything away from him. He'll still be a good person. He'll still be faithful to me, even if he has nothing."

So Satan took everything away from Job. His children and all the people who lived in his house died, and all of Job's things were gone too. Job was very sad, but he didn't get mad at God. Job knew that God was in charge. Job knew that God

loved him. It would have been easy for Job to give up on God. But Job knew he still wanted to be faithful to God.

God said to Satan, "See, Job is still faithful to me. Your plan didn't work."

"Well, if he were sick," said Satan, "he wouldn't be happy or faithful to you. It will be too hard for him, and he will give up on you."

God said, "Make him sick. He will be faithful to me." So, Satan made Job very sick. But Satan's plan didn't work. Job was still faithful to God even though he was very sick.

Job's wife was upset with him. "Why are you still faithful to God? It would be easier to give up on God. Just give up."

But Job said, "No, I'll be faithful to God. Sometimes bad things happen. I can't just give up on God. It's not that easy." Job still refused to give up on God, even if it was easier than being faithful.

Hear: All the people Job loved died, and he was very sad. Can you remember a time when you were very sad because you heard that someone you loved had died?

See: Which part of this story did you see in your imagination?

Act: Job lost a lot. What are some things that you think would be hard to give up?

God Remembers Job

Based on Selections from Job 19; 38

Sometimes, things happen to us that we don't understand. They can be good or bad things. It is really hard to understand why bad things happen to us.

Job had always been faithful to God. Even when he was sick and lost everything, he still loved God. Job's wife told him to give up on God. But Job refused. Then Job's friends came to visit him because they heard he was sick.

All of Job's friends thought that he must have done something wrong. God was good. If bad things were happening to Job, it was because God was punishing him. Job's friends told him, "God does bad things to bad people and good things to good people."

But Job knew that was not true. Sometimes, bad things happen to good people. Job knew that this was not what God did. Job knew that God was still with him, even though bad things had happened to him.

But Job still did not understand why these things were happening to him. He began to question God. God listened to Job's questions. "I know that it has been hard for you. But why do you question me? I am God. I have done many things that you do not know about. You cannot begin to understand what great things I have done."

Job thought about what God said. He thought about the things that had happened to him. He thought about how people had told him to give up on God. Sometimes, bad things happen in our lives, but God is still there. Job began to see that God was still good and that God still loved him. God loved him even when things happened that he didn't understand.

There are many people in our world who feel like God is punishing them, just like Job's friends told him. But even when we are sad or hurting, God is still with us and loves us.

Hear: What kinds of things do people say when bad things happen? Why do you think we have this book in the Bible?

See: We can't see God, so how do we know that God is still with us when we're sad or hurting?

Act: Tell a story about a time when you didn't think God was there.

God Asks Solomon a Question

Based on 1 Kings 3:1–15

If you could ask God for one thing, what would it be? King Solomon had that chance.

Solomon was a brand-new king. King David had ruled for many years. Now it was his son Solomon's turn. Solomon wanted to be a good king like his father, David. He decided to go to a place called Gibeon to pray. Lots of people went there to worship.

While Solomon was at Gibeon, God came to him in a dream: "Solomon, king of Israel, what do you want from me? Ask me for anything, and I will give it to you."

Solomon thought carefully about God's question. How should he answer?

"God," said Solomon, "You were kind to my father, King David. He followed in your ways and was a good king. Now you have made me king, but I feel so young. I don't know what I'm doing."

Solomon paused for a moment. Now he had to answer God's question. He wanted to ask for something to help him be a good king. What would be the best thing to ask for?

Suddenly Solomon had an idea. He knew how to answer God's question.

"Give me wisdom," Solomon said. "Then I can rule your people fairly. If I have your wisdom, I will know right from wrong. I will be able to see things the way that you see them. Then I will be a good king."

God was pleased that Solomon had asked for wisdom.

"You have chosen well," replied God. "You asked for wisdom to make the right decisions. I will give you what you asked. You will be the wisest person who has ever lived. I will also give you some things you did not ask for. You will have riches, and you will be famous. Now go, follow me, and keep my commandments. I will be with you forever, just as I was with your father, David."

Then Solomon woke up. He knew that God had spoken to him in a dream. He went back to his palace in Jerusalem and gave thanks to God.

Hear: How do you think Solomon knew that it was God speaking to him in his dream?

See: Imagine that Solomon's dream was made into a movie. What would the place where God and Solomon met look like?

Act: What kinds of things could you ask God to help you do?

Solomon Builds the Temple

Based on 1 Kings 6:1–38; 8:1–62

Have you ever watched a big building being built? Think about all the workers and materials needed. Solomon was in charge of a big building project.

King David wanted to build a house for God, but God said the time wasn't right. God promised that one of David's sons would build it instead.

Things were going well for King Solomon and the people of Israel. Finally peace was in the land. Solomon remembered God's promise to his father, King David. It was time to build the temple. It would be a place where the people worshiped God.

Solomon needed the best builders and artists to design and decorate the building. Solomon looked for the finest building materials too. It would be magnificent. It would be a house fit for God.

Skilled builders came from other lands to help. The king ordered cedarwood, fine stone, gold, and precious gems for them to use. Only the best was good enough for God's house. Solomon hired people to get the materials ready for building. Thousands of workers came to carve the stones and build the walls.

Then it was time to decorate the building. Artists covered the inside of the

temple with gold. They covered the altar with gold. They carved flowers and trees on the walls. The temple was beautiful inside and out.

Solomon built a special room inside the temple to hold the special chest. This chest was important to the people of God because it contained the Ten Commandments. It reminded them that God was with them.

It took seven years to finish the building. When it was ready, Solomon invited everyone to come to Jerusalem. People came from far and wide to worship God.

The priests brought the chest to the temple. They placed it in the special room. When they put the chest down, a bright cloud filled the building. God was in the cloud.

King Solomon prayed to God. He said thank you for all the things God had done. He asked God to look after the people and the temple. He asked God to listen when the people said they were sorry.

Solomon stood up and blessed the people, "May God always be with us. May God help us to walk in the ways of love."

Then Solomon and the people had a big party to celebrate the new temple.

Hear: Why do you think Solomon wanted to build the temple?

See: Imagine walking into the temple. What do you think it looked like?

Act: It's nice to have a special place to pray. Where do you like to pray?

The Fiery Furnace

Based on Daniel 3:8–30

Have you ever helped someone when others wouldn't? Then you made a choice to stand up for that person. Three young men had to make a choice to stand up for God in a foreign land. See what they decided to do.

The country of Babylon went to war with Israel. During the war, soldiers captured many Jewish people and took them back to Babylon. Among those taken were three young men named Shadrach, Meshach, and Abednego.

King Nebuchadnezzar was the ruler of Babylon. Everyone had to do what he said. One day, the king ordered his workers to build a huge golden statue. "Everyone must bow down and worship my statue," the king ordered. "I will punish anyone who does not bow down."

All the people obeyed and bowed down to the statue. That is, everyone except Shadrach, Meshach, and Abednego. They worshiped only God. When King Nebuchadnezzar heard about this, he was angry. "You must bow down to my statue," the king told the three men. "If you refuse I will throw you into a fiery furnace."

Shadrach, Meshach, and Abednego still would not bow down to the statue. The king was really angry! He told his soldiers to tie up the three young men and throw them into the fire.

Then an amazing thing happened! King Nebuchadnezzar looked into the furnace and saw four men walking around.

"We tied up three men and threw them into the blazing fire," the king said. "Now I see four men walking around in there. They are not tied up, and they are not hurt. One of them looks like a god!"

The king ordered Shadrach, Meshach, and Abednego to come out of the furnace. The three men walked out of the fire. They were not hurt, and their clothes were not burned. They didn't even smell like smoke!

King Nebuchadnezzar praised God for sending an angel to rescue the three men. He ordered everyone in Babylon to respect the God of Shadrach, Meshach, and Abednego.

Hear: How do you think the other Jewish captives felt when they heard that God saved Shadrach, Meshach, and Abednego? How might it make their faith stronger?

See: What do you think the fourth person in the furnace looked like?

Act: Have you ever been with a group that wanted you to do something wrong? How does it feel to stand up for what is right?

Prophets

Even though God found strong, faithful leaders, God's people forgot the covenant God had made with them many times. They forgot that God was their God, and they didn't follow God's ways. When that happened, God chose a prophet, a person to speak words from God to God's people. Often these words reminded the people that they were not following God and told them to change their ways. Not everyone God called wanted to be a prophet, but God didn't take no for an answer.

It wasn't easy to be a prophet for God, but God was always with each one, just as God promised. The last seventeen books of the Old Testament are books by and about the prophets. You can read about prophets in other books as well.

As you hear and read these stories about the prophets, pay attention to how God called them. What were they doing when they heard God's voice? Then notice how they responded.

One of the things you will see is that all these stories are about prophets who are men. However, you can find a story about a prophet named Deborah on page 72. It's different in our world, because prophets today can be both women and men.

As you read these stories about prophets God sent to the Israelites, think about what they were saying. God used prophets to tell the people things that God wanted them to remember. Who are prophets today who remind us about how we are to live together in love and care for all people? Who are prophets today who remind us about caring for our world? The work of the prophet in listening for God and speaking for God is as important today as it was in the biblical world.

Jonah Runs Away

Based on Jonah 1–2

Have you ever had a job that you really didn't want to do? Maybe you tried to forget about it or maybe you did it but you were mad about it. This is what happened to a man named Jonah. God gave him a job that he didn't want!

Jonah was a prophet of God. His job was to tell people what God told him. God said to Jonah, "Go to Nineveh and tell the people there to stop doing hurtful things. Tell them to say they are sorry, or I will punish them."

But Jonah didn't want to go. Jonah was from Israel, and people from Israel didn't like people from Nineveh. Instead of doing what God asked, Jonah ran the other way. He paid his way to sail on a ship. He thought this would put him farther away from God.

Out at sea, a huge, scary storm blew up. Waves crashed over the side of the ship. Everyone was afraid. They all started praying to their gods, except Jonah. He was fast asleep below the deck of the ship.

The captain found Jonah. He couldn't believe that Jonah was sleeping through the terrible storm. "What are you doing sleeping? Get up and pray!"

Jonah got up. He told everyone on the ship which god he worshiped. "I worship the Lord, the God of heaven."

The sailors thought that Jonah was running away from God. This scared them. Jonah said, "You're right. I'm running away from God. Throw me overboard, and the storm will stop."

The sailors tried to reach the shore, but they couldn't do it. Finally, they threw Jonah off the ship. At that moment, the storm stopped. The sailors worshiped Jonah's God.

But God was with Jonah. A big fish came and swallowed Jonah up. While he was inside the big fish, Jonah prayed to God. After three days, the big fish threw Jonah up onto dry land.

Hear: Have you ever been in a big storm? What did it sound like?

See: Can you imagine being inside a big fish? What would it look like inside?

Act: Have you ever wanted to run away from something that you knew you should do? Write a prayer that you could say to God when you feel like running away.

A Second Chance for Jonah

Based on Jonah 3–4

Do you know people who are really different from you? What makes them different? Is it their size? Is it the language they speak? Is it the color of their skin? Is it the place where they live? Is it how they look or act? This is the last part of the story of Jonah, who didn't want to be with people who were different from him. See what Jonah did and what God did.

Jonah needed a do-over, a try-again. The first time Jonah ran away and didn't listen to God. So God said, "Okay, Jonah, here's your second chance. Go to Nineveh and tell the people there to stop doing mean and hurtful things."

Jonah listened to God. He still didn't want to go to Nineveh, but this time he went. "God says you have forty days to stop being mean, or you will be punished," Jonah said grumpily.

Amazingly, everyone listened! Everyone in Nineveh, even the king, stopped being mean and listened to God. God was so happy that God's mind changed. God didn't punish the people of Nineveh.

The people of Nineveh listened! Jonah did his job. What a great prophet! But Jonah was not happy. "Ugh, I know God is good and merciful. But did God have to be so kind to the people of Nineveh? I don't like them at all! This is why I ran away. I'm angry!"

God saw that Jonah was angry. God said, "Oh, come on, Jonah. Is it really right to be angry about this?"

Jonah stormed off. God thought, *Hmm, this is a good time to teach Jonah why I care about the people of Nineveh.* God made a big bush grow. Jonah sat in its shade. Jonah was very comfortable. Then God sent a worm to eat the bush. Jonah got even angrier when the bush was gone. He threw a big fit. He shouted, "I'm so angry that I don't even want to be alive!"

God chuckled and said, "Oh, Jonah, is it really right to be this upset about a bush? Don't be silly. If you can care this much about a bush, how can you be mad at me for caring so much about the people of Nineveh?"

Hear: Why do you think the people listened to Jonah? Who do you listen to?

See: What do you hear in this story that you would like to draw?

Act: Have you ever walked away from something that you knew you should do? Did you get a second chance? Write a story about second chances.

What Are You Doing Here?

Based on 1 Kings 19:1–21

Sometimes bad things happen, and you just want to run away and hide or start over. This is what happened to one of God's prophets named Elijah. He thought he could hide from God, but God found him.

Queen Jezebel was very angry. Elijah had ordered all her priests to be killed because they were worshiping gods that weren't real. Elijah was a prophet. His name means "My God is Yahweh." He was trying to do everything he could to be sure the Israelites knew that God was the real, true God. Sometimes that was a dangerous and scary job. Jezebel threatened Elijah, so he ran away to save his life.

Elijah ran to the wilderness. Everything with Jezebel was so scary. All Elijah could think to do was pray, "Oh God, let me die. I've failed trying to teach people that you

are the real, true God." While he was praying, he fell asleep. He woke up when an angel gently touched him and said, "Get up and eat."

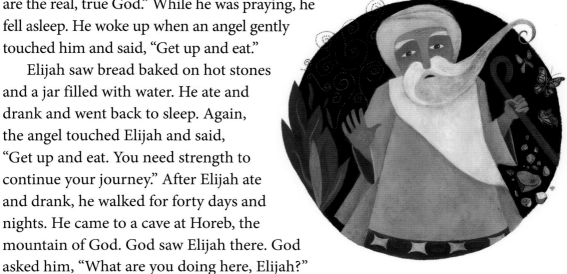

Elijah saw bread baked on hot stones and a jar filled with water. He ate and drank and went back to sleep. Again, the angel touched Elijah and said, "Get up and eat. You need strength to continue your journey." After Elijah ate and drank, he walked for forty days and nights. He came to a cave at Horeb, the mountain of God. God saw Elijah there. God asked him, "What are you doing here, Elijah?"

Elijah replied, "I've been trying to do the right thing, telling people that you are the real God. But they just don't get it. Now they want to kill me."

A great wind came. It was so strong that it tore mountains apart and broke rocks into little pieces. God was not in the wind.

Then an earthquake shook the cave. God was not in the earthquake.

Then a fire. God was not in the fire.

Finally, it was completely silent.

Elijah wrapped his coat around his face. He went to the cave's entrance. A voice said, "Elijah, what are you doing here?"

Elijah said, "God, I really have tried very hard. But the people aren't listening."

God said, "Go to Damascus. There people will help you. Tell them that they will have holy jobs that God has chosen for them. I'll take care of Israel."

Elisha was plowing a field with twelve oxen when Elijah found him. Elijah walked by and threw his coat over Elisha. What could that mean? Elisha knew what it meant. He ran after Elijah. "Let me say good-bye to my parents. Then I'll come with you and help you."

Elisha went back and prepared a meal for his family. Then Elisha went with Elijah.

Hear: What does complete silence sound like? Can you describe it?

See: Who do you see who is trying hard to do what God wants them to do?

Act: What things can you do that show you love God?

I Will Not Leave You

Based on 2 Kings 2:1–15

This is a story about two good friends and what happened to them. Reading it helps us remember how God was always with God's people, loving and caring for them.

Elijah and Elisha had a very special friendship. It was almost like Elisha was Elijah's son. Elijah taught Elisha everything he knew about the world and about God.

They were on a journey together. They both knew that Elijah was going to die that day. Elijah said to Elisha, "Stay here. God wants me to go all the way to Bethel."

But Elisha said, "As long as God lives and as long as you live, I won't leave you."

A group of prophets met them in Bethel. They said to Elisha, "Don't you know that Elijah is going to die today?"

Elisha said, "Yes, I know. But don't talk about it."

Elijah said, "Elisha, stay here. God wants me to go all the way to Jericho."

But Elisha said, "As long as God lives and as long as you live, I won't leave you."

They went to Jericho. A group of prophets who were there met them. They said to Elisha, "Don't you know that Elijah is going to die today?"

Elisha replied, "Yes, I know. But don't talk about it."

Elijah turned to Elisha. He said, "Stay here. God is sending me to Jordan."

But Elisha said again, "As long as God lives and as long as you live, I won't leave you."

They kept going. Fifty prophets joined them. When they got to the Jordan River, the prophets stood away from Elijah and Elisha. Elijah took off his coat, rolled it up, and hit the river. The water separated. Some water went to one side. The rest went to the other side. A path was made. Elijah and Elisha could walk on dry ground to the other side of the river.

Together they crossed the river. Elijah said to Elisha, "What can I do for you before I'm taken away today?"

Elisha said, "I look up to you so much. Leave your spirit with me."

Elijah said, "That's a tough one. If you can see me when I'm taken from you, then it will happen. But if you can't see me, it won't happen."

They kept walking and talking. Suddenly, a chariot and horses made of fire swooped down. Elijah and Elisha were separated. Elijah went to heaven in a big gust of wind. Elisha screamed, "My father, my father!"

Elisha grabbed his clothes and tore them in half. Then he picked up Elijah's coat. He hit the water with it. He yelled, "Where is Elijah's God now?"

The water separated to make a path on dry ground. Elisha walked to the other side of the Jordan River.

The group of prophets saw all this. They were amazed. "Wow, the spirit of Elijah really is with Elisha," they said.

As Elisha walked up, they bowed down before him.

Hear: How would you feel if you heard that someone you knew was going to die?

See: Sometimes things that happen are hard to believe. Have you ever seen anything happen that was hard to believe was real?

Act: How could you care for someone who has lost someone they love?

Elisha the Healer

Based on 2 Kings 5:1–19

When this story was written, people didn't go to doctors like we do today. Instead, they went to healers. Elisha was a prophet who healed people.

Naaman was a powerful general in the king's army. He was a good man. But there was something wrong with his skin. Scabs and sores covered his body. Naaman needed help. He needed his body to be healed.

A young woman had been brought from Israel by the army. She worked for Naaman's wife. The young woman said, "Your husband's skin can be healed. I know who can help him. It is the prophet Elisha who lives in Samaria."

Naaman went to Samaria to find the prophet. Elisha was at home when Naaman showed up with his horses and chariots. Elisha sent a servant to talk to him. The servant said, "Wash yourself in the Jordan River seven times. Then your skin will be healthy and clean."

Naaman, the big, powerful general, did not like that message. He stormed off, muttering, "I came all this way to see Elisha, the healer, and he just sends a servant to me? I'm an important general! Elisha should come out and heal me himself. I don't want to hear silly instructions from his servant!"

One of Naaman's servants followed him. He bravely asked, "If the prophet had said to do something really hard, you would have done it, right? Why not do this really easy thing and be healed? Go on. Take seven baths in the Jordan River and see what happens."

Naaman listened. He went to the Jordan River. Naaman bathed in it seven times. When he came out, the scabs and sores were gone. Naaman's skin was healthy and clean!

Naaman sent for Elisha, and said, "I didn't think it would work, but it did. Now I know that the God you believe in is real. You are a powerful and important prophet!"

Naaman tried to give Elisha gifts to say thank you. Elisha said, "No, I will not accept your gifts."

Naaman went away thankful for clean and healthy skin. And he believed in God.

Hear: What words do you like to hear when you feel sick?

See: What do you do when you see someone who looks sick?

Act: We can't all heal people like Elisha could, but we can be kind to people who are sick. What can you do for someone who is sick?

Telling the Truth

Based on Amos 1:1; 4:13; 5:14–15; 7:12

Have you ever seen someone treated unfairly at school? On the playground? This story is about God's prophet Amos. He wanted people to look around and see what was going on. He told them hard things that were true. But the people didn't want to hear them.

Amos grew up in a small village in Judah. He and his family were farmers. Every day they took care of their fields and their animals.

"God makes the mountains, creates the wind, cares about each of us, and helps the sun to rise in the morning," Amos said. Perhaps he was remembering his early mornings taking care of the farm with his family. Amos believed deeply that God was good and fair.

When people weren't treated fairly, Amos got angry. He did not like it that some people had so much while others had so little. When he saw bad things happening, he shouted to the people in Israel, "You rich people are making the poor people feel like dirt. You think you are fancy and better than everyone else. Stop wasting your money on things that do not matter when people need money for food and clothes and a place to live!"

The rich people did not like what Amos said. Amos was kicked out of Israel. "The things you are saying are just too hard to hear. We can't handle them. Go home to Judah. Don't ever come here again," they told Amos.

Amos replied, "I am a farmer. I did not want to come here. God told me to come and tell you the truth."

Amos cared about people. He wanted everyone to be treated fairly. Amos told everyone, "Try to do good things, not evil things. Take care of each other. God will be with you."

Hear: Who do you know who tells the truth even when it's hard?

See: What do you see in the world that makes you angry?

Act: What's one thing you can do to help someone else?

143

What Does God Want?

Based on Micah 1:1; 4:1–4; 6:6–8

Sometimes we need people to help us see what's going on. It's good when someone points out ways we can live as God wants, loving and caring for others. Micah was a prophet who helped people see how God wanted them to live together.

Micah was from a small village outside Jerusalem. He grew up in a family of farmers. He spent every day in vineyards and fields. Sometimes people in these villages were treated badly by rich, powerful people in the cities. Micah knew this was wrong.

He traveled to the big city of Jerusalem and said, "God doesn't want rich and powerful people to treat poor or powerless people badly."

Images of fields and trees from his village filled his mind. All Micah could think about was the time he spent plowing and picking the grain with family and friends.

"When the world is filled with peace, people will beat their weapons into farm tools. No one will make war. We will all sit under our grapevines and fig trees," Micah told the people in Jerusalem.

Micah knew what it was like to be poor. He knew deep down inside what it was like to be treated terribly by people who had power and money. He had big ideas about how God wanted people to treat one another.

Like other prophets, Micah had a difficult job. He had to speak hard truths to God's people. Truths that they did not want to hear about how powerful and rich people treated others unfairly. Micah talked about the destruction that was coming if God's people ignored how God wanted them to treat one another.

What God really wanted was for people to:

do justice,

love kindness,

and walk humbly with God.

That's how Micah said it. Now think about what it means for you!

You are doing justice when you make sure that everyone is treated fairly.

You love kindness when you share something that is really precious to you.

When you walk with your eyes open to see places where you and your family can help someone—like a refugee or someone who is sick or hungry or needs money to buy school supplies—then you are walking humbly with God.

Micah believed with all his heart that this is what God wanted everyone to do. And we can choose to live our lives this way today.

Hear: What do you want to remember about the message that God gave to the prophet Micah?

See: What would the world look like if there were no weapons that could harm people? What would a peaceful world look like?

Act: How can you spread Micah's message about peace and caring for one another?

You Are Not Alone

Based on Isaiah 43:1–7

Have you ever been afraid? Everyone is afraid sometimes. That's okay. The people who heard the words God gave Isaiah knew what it was like to be afraid. They were living in a very scary time. They were forced to leave their homes, and they weren't allowed to go back.

Some people felt as if their whole world was ending. What was going to happen? Would they ever be able to go home? Did God even love them anymore?

Isaiah wanted to give God's people hope and encouragement. God had this message for them: "Do not be afraid. I am with you. I know your name, and you are special to me. When you get into the water, I will be with you. I will not let the water get too high. When you walk through fire, you won't be burned because I will be with you. I am God. You are so special. And I love you. I will bring you home again and make sure that you stay safe."

God knew that their lives were hard. Isaiah's job as a prophet was to bring these words to God's people. One day they were written down so that everyone would

know that God is with them no matter what. Even when bad things happen, God is there with us. We don't have to do anything alone. God is with us even during the scariest times.

Hear: What words help you when you are afraid? What would you want to hear God say to you when you are afraid?

See: God's words bring comfort. Which of God's messages would you like to see when you wake up each morning?

Act: Choose a sentence from God's words to the people. Write them on a sheet of paper and decorate it. Display it where your family will see it.

Speak Up, Jeremiah

Based on Jeremiah 1:1–10; 31:31–34

Have you ever felt like you had something really important to say, but you didn't know how to say it? What if you say the wrong thing? Or someone gets mad? It can be scary to speak up, even when you know it is important.

Jeremiah was a prophet. A prophet is someone who delivers God's message to God's people. Jeremiah worried that he didn't have the right words to say to God's people. God said, "Jeremiah, I know you. I knew you even before you were born. You can say these important words to my people."

But Jeremiah was scared. "Oh no, I don't think I can do it. I don't know how to talk like that," he said to God.

God knew that Jeremiah was the right person for the job. God said to Jeremiah, "Go. Speak. Do not be afraid. I am with you. I will help you find the right words."

Jeremiah listened and trusted God. Being a prophet was not an easy job. Jeremiah spoke hard words to God's people. Some people became angry. They didn't want to hear Jeremiah telling them that they were not being kind to one another. "Change your ways. Say you're sorry. Listen to God," Jeremiah said.

Some people hit Jeremiah. He was put in jail and then pushed down to the bottom of a muddy well. But Jeremiah didn't give up. He knew that he was doing the right thing. He knew he needed to be God's voice. God was with him. God also had a message of hope for the people. Jeremiah told them, "God is going to make a new promise with you. This promise will be for everyone, the youngest and the oldest. God promises to love all of you. You are God's people, each and every one of you. God will forgive you."

Hear: What do you think Jeremiah sounded like when he gave God's message to the people? Try to draw it or paint it.

See: What do you see around you that reminds you of God's promise to love you?

Act: God loves you, and you are one of God's people. Name three ways that you can show God's love to others.

Songs and Wise Sayings

Many books in the Old Testament tell stories about God and God's people. A few are books of instructions about how to live in God's way. Still others are books that look like poetry, and they are. The book of Psalms contains poems that were the songs of God's people in Old Testament times and centuries later. Today we read them like poetry, and many of the hymns we sing in church are based on them. The books of Proverbs and Ecclesiastes are also poems that provide instructions.

There are many kinds of psalms, and you'll read some of them here. In some psalms, the writer is saying thank you to God or "Wow, that's amazing," which is like a psalm of praise to God. In other psalms, the writer is thinking about how she trusts God and how God cares for the earth. And then there are psalms where the writer is expressing sadness and asking for help. All these different kinds of psalms are just like feelings we have today: joy and happiness, sadness and hoping for something different, and thanksgiving. It's good to know that we can always tell God our hopes and concerns.

The writers of Proverbs and Ecclesiastes provide both instructions and things for us to remember. As you read the stories from these kinds of writings that are like poetry and instruction books, you might try writing your own as you think about how God wants you to live.

Thank You, God!

Based on Psalm 100

When someone gives you a gift, you usually say thank you. You can do that with words, or hugs, or even with a picture or a card. But how do you say thank you to God? It is hard to hug God or draw a picture for God. We can say thank you with a prayer.

The book of the Bible called the Psalms has 150 poems. Many of the poems were the words for songs to God. Many of the poems are prayers. Some psalms

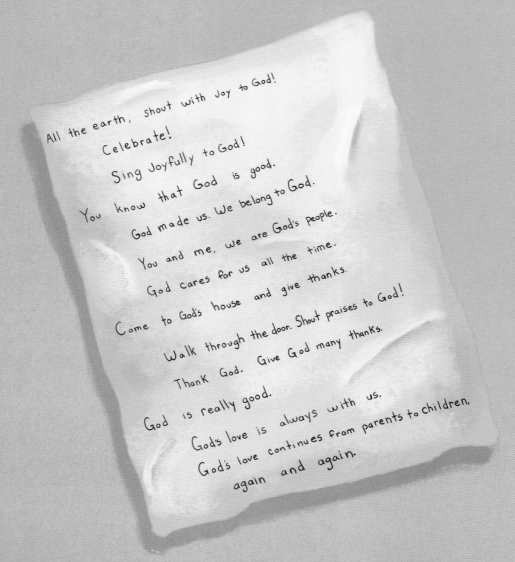

All the earth, shout with Joy to God!
Celebrate!
Sing joyfully to God!
You know that God is good.
God made us. We belong to God.
You and me, we are God's people.
God cares for us all the time.
Come to God's house and give thanks.
Walk through the door. Shout praises to God!
Thank God. Give God many thanks.
God is really good.
God's love is always with us.
God's love continues from parents to children,
again and again.

say thank you to God for the world and the people that God created. Here is one thank-you poem.

Hear: What is the nicest thing someone has said about you? Could you say that about God too?

See: Draw a picture of something God has made for which you are thankful.

Act: Ask your family members to tell you what they thank God for. Use their answers to write a prayer your family can pray together.

Help Me, God!

Based on Psalm 28

When you need help with something like homework or learning to pitch a ball or ride a bike, who helps you? When you make a mistake, who helps you learn how to do better next time? Perhaps you ask a parent or grandparent, aunt or uncle, teacher or neighbor to help because you know that they love you. Because we know that God loves us, we can ask God for help, too. God may not teach us how to ride a bike, but God can help us be kind and loving.

The book of the Bible called the Psalms is a book of poems and prayers. Some of them ask God for help. They show us how we can ask God for help. This poem-prayer is based on verses from Psalm 28.

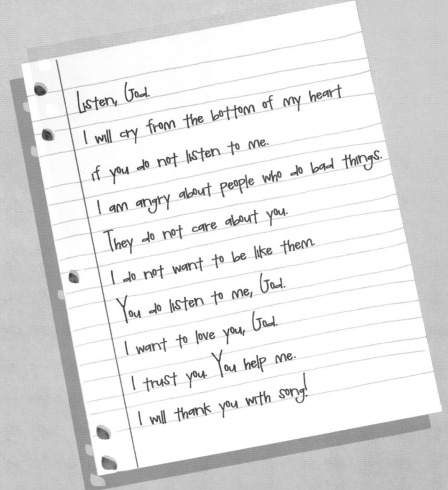

Listen, God.
I will cry from the bottom of my heart
if you do not listen to me.
I am angry about people who do bad things.
They do not care about you.
I do not want to be like them.
You do listen to me, God.
I want to love you, God.
I trust you. You help me.
I will thank you with song!

Hear: What do you think this prayer means?

See: How have you seen people pray? What can you do with your hands and face when you pray?

Act: What help would you ask God for? Can you draw a picture and show it to an adult you trust?

I Love You, God!

Based on Psalm 23

In the book of Psalms, some prayers help us tell God that we love God. Some of the prayers help us talk to God. They tell us that we can trust God. Have you ever wondered how to say, "I love you" to God? This psalm is a good example. King David may have written this psalm when he was a shepherd. He spent days and nights with the sheep. We tell God, "I love you," and we know that God already loves us.

God takes care of me
like a shepherd cares for the sheep.
I have everything I need:
food to eat,
and water to drink.
God takes care of me.
God leads me to good ways of living.

Even when I am frightened,
I remember that God is with me.
God cares for me and keeps me safe.

God, you care for me.
even when people want to be mean to me.
You give more than I can imagine.
Yes, your constant love will be with me forever.
I will be your child as long as I live.

Hear: How does David tell God "I love you" in this psalm?

See: How have you seen people tell God "I love you"? Can you tell God this without words?

Act: Make a valentine for God. Where will you keep your valentine?

Right and Wrong

Based on Proverbs 10

How do you know to do the right thing? Who do you learn from? Proverbs is a collection of things to remember. Jewish people used them to teach their children and one another. Proverbs helped the people learn more about who God wanted them to be and what to do. In these proverbs, we meet Wise, Silly, Bad, and Good. Through them we see how we are responsible for what we do. They help us see how we are a mix of bad and good: Bad and good words. Bad and good things we do toward other living things. And bad and good things we think in our heads. Each proverb (each line) is one idea.

Wise listens to make Wise's parents proud. Silly makes Silly's parents sad.

Bad does things that are wrong. God won't listen to Bad. But Good will be heard by God.

Wise works hard. Silly sleeps all day.

Good is loved by God. Bad doesn't tell the truth.

Wise listens to instructions. Silly talks and pays no attention to what anyone is saying.

Good tries to do the right thing. Bad tries to hide wrong behavior.

Wise listens to other people. Silly talks a lot.

Wise learns from mistakes. Silly ignores instructions.

Silly does not speak with love. Wise does not talk too much.

Good cares for other people. Silly does not.

When everything is upside down, God will care for Good.

Good finds joy in life. Bad is unhappy.

Good will tell the truth. Bad will be silent.

Wise does the right thing. Bad only does what is wrong.

Hear: When have you acted like one of these characters? Which one? What did you do?

See: If you were going to act out one of these proverbs, what would you wear to be each character?

Act: If you were going to write a proverb to teach something, what would you say?

A Time for Everything!

Based on Ecclesiastes 3:1–7

You do many things in just one day. You might go to school. Some days you go to the doctor's office or the grocery store. Maybe you read every day. Many days you help with chores around the house. Ecclesiastes has wise sayings to help you understand the rhythm of life. As new things happen in your life, you have different feelings. Some times make you sad. Other times make you happy. It may help you to know that each time brings its own feeling.

There is a time for everything.
There is a time for you to make new things
    and a time to tear things down.
There is a time for you to welcome
    and a time to say good-bye.
There is a time to get ready
    and a time to stop.
There is a time when you are hurt
    and a time when you get better.
There is a time when you cry
    and a time when you laugh.
There is a time when you are sad
    and a time when you dance with joy.
There is a time to look for someone or something
    and a time to hide.
There is a time to listen
    and a time to talk.
There is a time to be angry
    and a time to love.

Hear: Which of these times have you experienced? How did you feel during each one?

See: If you were going to draw one of these verses, what colors would you use?

Act: How could you use these words to make a card for someone who is sad, or angry, or hurt?

Listening for God

The Old Testament has a collection of many stories and many different kinds of writing. Could it all be telling one story? Think about the Old Testament as being like a very large quilt. It is made up of many different colors and kinds of fabrics. There are threads that run throughout the different squares, threads that tie the stories together. What do you think?

Here are some stories that will help you remember how you are to live with God's voice inside you. It's amazing to think that these really old stories still speak to us today, so many centuries later.

The story of the people who wanted to stay together and be all alike is really a story about God's plan for us to learn how to live with difference. Rules help us remember how we are to live. The Ten Commandments remind us of how we are to love God and love and treat other people. Some people want to know if one commandment is the greatest, and we learn about that in Deuteronomy.

Throughout the stories in the Bible, we hear names and metaphors, or symbols, for God. We read stories about people who met God in light and dark, in storms and fire, in wind and rainbows. Some people met God in silence, and others met God in other people. These stories remind us that whether we call God mother or father, shepherd or healer, God hears all the names we use, all the prayers we say. The Old Testament is full of stories of people meeting God. These stories remind us that God still meets us today in some of the very same places.

God's Big Plan

Based on Genesis 11:1–9

How did we get to be so different? Wouldn't it be easier if we were all alike? Here's the story of God's people who were all alike and liked it that way. Then God surprised them.

After the flood, the children, grandchildren, and great-grandchildren of Noah were one big family. They moved to Shinar, where the world started over again after the great flood. They all spoke the same language and lived together in one place.

They said, "Let's build a big city with a very tall skyscraper here so that we can stay together." They liked living in a city where everyone knew everyone else. They liked speaking the same language. They liked being all alike. And they didn't want to leave.

God saw them building their city and their skyscraper. God said, "They're one big family. They're all alike. And they're all speaking the same language. If I don't do something, things will never change. Everyone will be just like everyone else forever."

So God came up with two new ideas for these children, and grandchildren, and

great-grandchildren of Noah. First, God gave them different languages to speak. Then God sent them out to live in different places all over the whole world.

The people never finished building their city. They could have called it Many-town, because that's where the people living in many places and speaking many languages came from. But they called it Babel. That was their word for dividing one language into many languages. It was their word for dividing one place into the many places where we all live in the world today.

The people building Babel had a little plan to stay together. But God had a big plan that was different. God wanted to fill the world with different languages, different people, and different ways of living.

And that's what God did.

Hear: What language do you think the people of the city of Babel spoke? What did it sound like? What languages do people speak where you live?

See: What did the people of the city of Babel look like? What do people look like where you live? Do they all look the same, or do they look different?

Act: How are people alike, and how are they different where you live?

God Gives the Ten Commandments

Based on Exodus 20:1–21

What rules do you have to follow when you are at home and school? The Israelites had some special rules, too. This is the story about how they got them.

One day the Hebrew people camped near a mountain. God wanted Moses to come up the mountain. God had a message for Moses to give to the people.

Moses told everyone to gather at the bottom of the mountain. "God has something important to say," Moses explained. "Wait here, and you will be able to hear God speak."

The people stood at the bottom of the mountain and waited. Suddenly, the earth began to shake. A thick cloud of smoke came down over the mountain. Thunder clapped and lightening flashed. A trumpet blew loudly. God was on the mountain.

Moses climbed up into the cloud of smoke to meet with God. God gave Moses ten important rules to help the people live in loving ways. They were written on two stone slabs.

The first four rules were about God.

1. There is only one God.
2. Remember I am your God. Worship only me.
3. When you say my name, speak it with love and respect.
4. Remember the Sabbath on the seventh day of the week. Work on the other six days and rest on the seventh. Make it a day set apart for me.

The other six rules were about how to live with other people.

5. Treat your father and your mother with respect. Look after them.
6. Don't kill anyone. Respect all people.
7. Be true to your husband or wife.
8. Don't take the things that belong to others.
9. Don't lie about anyone. Always tell the truth.
10. Don't wish you had things that belong to other people. Be happy with the things you have.

The people heard the thunder and the trumpet. They saw the lightning and the cloud of smoke. They were afraid and moved away from the mountain.

"Don't be afraid," Moses said. "God just wants you to know how to live so that you won't do the wrong things."

Hear: How do you think God's special rules helped the people live more fairly with one another? What would happen in the world if everyone followed these rules?

See: Moses climbed the mountain to meet with God. What do you think Moses saw at the top of the mountain?

Act: Where do you see people following God's special rules today? Which of these rules have you followed in the past week? What can you do differently so that you can follow God's rules?

The Most Important Thing to Remember

Based on Deuteronomy 6:4–9

There are so many things you have to remember: Eat healthy snacks. Brush your teeth before bed. Look both ways before crossing the street. And then there are the really important things to remember, about how God wants us to live in the world.

Try saying this: *Shema Yisrael*. It's Hebrew, and it means "Hear, O Israel." It's so important that Jewish people say it twice a day, when they wake up and when they go to bed. This small part of the book of Deuteronomy is called the *Shema*. It helps Jews and Christians remember what is most important for how we live in the world.

So here's what we are being asked to hear and remember:

Listen, Our God is the Lord. Don't think anything or anyone else can be your God.

Love God with your heart.

Love God with everything you have.

Remember these words.

Tell them to your children.

Remember to love God everywhere—when you are away from home, and when you are at home. Remember them when you get up in the morning and when you go to sleep at night.

If you can't remember these words, then write them down so that you won't forget. You can even write them on a stone and put it outside your front door.

So that's it. Pretty simple, right? God wants us to remember that we belong to God. And God loves us so much. God wants us to love God back. It makes you think about all the ways we can show God how big our love is.

Hear: How does it sound when you say "Hear, O Israel" in Hebrew, *Shema Yisrael*?

See: Where might you write *Shema Yisrael* so that you will see it when you wake up and when you go to sleep?

Act: What are some ways you can love God back?

Love the Lord your God

Love the Lord your God

Love the Lord your God

What Is God's Name?

Based on Exodus 3:14; Psalm 23; Isaiah 30:23; 54:13

Names have been important since the beginning of time. In Genesis, one of the most important jobs Adam had was to name the animals. As humans, we are all given names when we're born. We even name our pets! What is your name? Do you have a nickname? What is your pet's name? Names are important because they help us know who we are. We all have several names. So does God!

Some writers of the Old Testament called God by the name *Yahweh*. *Yahweh* is the name for God, which means "I Am Who I Am." *Adonai* and *El Shaddai* are other Hebrew names for God. They mean "Lord." Lord is a name given to powerful rulers. This is exactly what many believed God to be.

But "Lord" isn't the only name for God used by the Old Testament writers. They also call God "Shepherd," a job held by people who cared for sheep. That is quite different from Lord, isn't it? "Provider" was another name given to God. It is a way to say "thank you" for all things: food, family, safety, and love. People also called God "Peacemaker." Perhaps they used this name because people felt close to God in times of peace. When have you felt peaceful? Did you feel God in that moment?

In one story, Moses asked about God's name. God replied simply, "I Am Who I Am." What do you think that could mean?

Why do you think so many names were given to God? I wonder if it's because God is so big that one name couldn't possibly be enough. Or maybe God has lots of characteristics that needed to be written about. What do you think?

Hear: Think about the names for God you've heard at church. What names for God are sung in the songs and hymns? What names are spoken in prayers and liturgies?

See: What name do you like to call God?

Act: What are some ways you could help God by being a peacemaker?

What Is God Like?

Based on 2 Samuel 22:47; Psalm 23; Matthew 23:37

My eyes are blue like the ocean. You are the light of the world.

Okay, so my eyes aren't *actually* like the ocean—but they *are* blue. We are not *actually* walking, talking candles or flashlights—but we can bring joy and warmth to the world, just like a light. What are *you* like?

People who wrote the books in the Bible did call God by name. But sometimes, names weren't enough to describe God. These writers often needed another way to talk about God. So they used words that the people who read the Bible would know. These words are familiar to us even today. They are called *metaphors* because they help people know what God is like. Here are a few:

God is like a *mother* and a *father*. Many times, God is said to be like a mother, comforting God's children. Like a mother hen, God protects her children. Jesus called God his father.

Shepherd is another image used to write about the ways God works in the world. God guides, leads, and provides for God's "sheep" (us!).

Rocks are strong. Writers wanted people to know that God was strong. This image helped people remember that God's love for them was like a *strong rock*, always there. Like a rock, God protects people.

And then there's the image of *breath* in the Bible. Your breath is usually invisible, unless you see it when you breathe out in cold weather. But your breath is close to you. It's inside you, keeping you alive. Do you think that's why the Old Testament writers used *breath* as a metaphor for God?

At the very beginning in Genesis, we know that God gave *light* to the world. Light is needed by every living thing to grow and thrive. Many of the writers of the Psalms tell us about God's light. David wrote that God was his light and the One who took care of him.

This list could go on forever and ever. But one thing we can learn from all these images and metaphors is this: God is BIG, and sometimes words are not enough. What is God like for you?

Hear: Notice the sounds around you. What do you hear that might be a way to describe God?

See: What words do *you* use to describe God?

Act: How can you be like water and light, soothing and life-giving to your friends and family?

How Close Is God?

Based on Genesis 9:12–17; 28:10–15; Exodus 13:20–22; 19:19; 1 Kings 19:11–12

"**S**nuggle up, get real close." Did anyone ever say that to you? It feels good to be close, especially when it's really cold or dark.

Do you think God is very close to you? Or do you think God is far away? Isn't it hard to think about God? We can't just reach out and touch God. It's easier to think about being close to a parent, a friend, or even your dog. In the Bible are stories about times when people felt close to God.

God is very close when. . .

You see a rainbow. Sometimes after the rain you look at the sky, and there is a beautiful rainbow. It reminds us of the story of Noah. After the flood, God

promised Noah that the whole world would not be flooded again. When you see a rainbow, remember God is close.

You hear thunder. You know a storm is coming when you hear thunder. What do you do when you hear it? God called Moses to go up Mount Sinai so that God could give him the Ten Commandments. God's voice was thunder. David writes about God's voice in Psalm 29. He says that God's voice is thunder, very strong and loud.

It is very quiet. What does silence sound like? It's very different from thunder, isn't it? Elijah was running from Jezebel and ended up on a mountain. He thought he would be close to God in the wind or the earthquake or a fire. But then it was quiet, no noise at all! And Elijah felt close to God in the silence.

You see clouds and fire. When Moses was leading God's people out of slavery into freedom, Moses wondered how they would find their way out of Egypt. God led the way with clouds during the daytime. At night, when they looked up at the sky, lightening that looked like fire lit the sky to help them see the way.

You dream. Jacob had a dream about stairs that went from the ground all the way to the sky. Then he saw God standing next to him. God said, "I will always be with you. I will never leave you."

Hear: Have you ever had a dream like Jacob's?

See: Where do you feel close to God?

Act: Find a quiet space. Listen for God's voice speaking to you.

Where Does God Live?

Based on Exodus 3:1-6; Psalm 29:3; Matthew 3:16; Acts 2:2

When someone asks you where you live, you might say, "4197 Daisy Lane" or "Tennessee" or "in a yellow house." But where does God live?

The Bible tells us that God has many homes and can be found in many places, often where we least expect. God is found in the beauty and magnificence of nature—in thunder, in fire and bushes, in the wind, and in a peaceful dove. Jesus often traveled into the wilderness to listen for God's voice. He knew that God could be found in nature.

Many of the words used to describe God in the Bible also give clues to where God might be found: breath, light, mother, father, water, bread of life. These images are like a pin in a map, giving us great ideas of where to look for God. *Breath*, *mother*, and *father* suggest that God lives very, very close to us. God is in our homes, in the people we love the most, and in our own bodies. *Light* and *water* tell us that God lives near the earth. From the highest heights to the deepest depths, God moves,

connecting us all to one another. *Bread of Life* helps us to see God in simple moments like sitting around the dinner table sharing a meal with family or friends.

Solomon built a house for God, and we do the same today. People who love God build sanctuaries and synagogues, mosques and gurdwaras, places where they can be close to God. God doesn't live there, but we feel God's love when we are there.

But God isn't just found in people or things. God is also found in love. We know that God is the source of love. That means that when we treat one another with love, God is there. The best way to discover God's "address" is to love yourself and others well. When you love like that, you will find God.

Do you have a sense that God is in nature when you play outside and feel the warm sun on your back? Perhaps you feel God's presence when your parent tucks you in at night or when your friend gives you a big hug. No matter where else God might live, one thing is certain: God lives in you.

Hear: Put your head on your parent's chest and listen to the heartbeat. That is a God-sound!

See: Where else do you think God lives?

Act: What are some ways you can be a strong home for God's presence?

Please Remember! Never Forget!

Y ou probably have a lot of things to remember that parents and teachers and other adults tell you. Look both ways before crossing the street. Be smart with your choices. Eat healthy snacks. Be kind to others. So many things to remember!

If you have read through the stories in the Old Testament section of this Bible storybook, you know that God wanted the people to remember a lot of things. Take a minute and think about what you have heard in the stories and seen in the pictures.

From the beginning with the first story of God making everything, we know that God wants us to take care of the world and keep it beautiful. The story of Noah and his family reminds us that God will always keep us safe. God's big plan tells us that we are all different. We speak different languages. We eat different kinds of food, and we have different ways of celebrating. God created us this way and wants us to learn how to live together in peace.

From the stories about Jacob and Esau, Sarah and Hagar, and Joseph and his brothers, we know that sometimes it is hard to be kind and to do loving things for others. It was hard for people in the Old Testament, and it's still hard for us today. Even though we don't always get things right, God forgives us and wants us never to forget that.

Remember the stories about Ruth and Naomi, Deborah, David, and Esther? They remind us how important it is to be a good friend, to be a wise leader!

And you read about some of God's prophets: Amos, Micah, Isaiah, and Jeremiah. Their words from God help us remember how important it is to care for others and to work to make the world a better place for everyone.

All these stories have some things in common. They help us know that God's heart is very big. God loves us very much. God wants us to show God's love to everyone we meet. Please remember! Never forget!

Hear: Which Old Testament stories were your favorites? Which stories were new to you? Which ones had you heard before?

See: Use your eyes this week. Where do you see people doing kind things? Where do you see people doing hard things? Where do you see people doing smart things? Where do you see people showing God's love?

Act: What are some ways you can share God's love?

Please Remember

Never Forget

New
Testament

Introduction to the New Testament

Some people use pictures and words to make scrapbooks about things they want to remember. Maybe you have a baby book with words and pictures. It tells about your birth or adoption and the first years of your life. Or instead of a baby book, you might have a file on the family computer with all kinds of pictures.

The stories in the first four books in this section of our Bible are like a big album, full of pictures. Each story adds a picture that tells us about Jesus: how he lived, what he taught, and what we need to remember. The stories in the first four books were written by Matthew, Mark, Luke, and John. Each of them wrote in their own way to tell their stories about Jesus. You'll hear stories about how Jesus used parables to teach about God. And there are stories about how he healed people with his words and his touch. When Jesus taught and when he healed people, he wanted them to think about how they could live with one another.

Jesus met a lot of interesting people: Peter, Mary and Martha, Joanna and Susanna, and Zacchaeus. And there are stories about some people whose names we don't even know. Each person was different after meeting Jesus.

After Jesus died and was alive again, he left the earth. And everyone who knew him had to decide how to start all over again, living the way Jesus taught. Luke also wrote another book. It's called the Acts of the Apostles. It tells stories about the beginnings of the church. Here you'll meet people like Philip and Paul, Tabitha, Lydia, and Timothy. As you hear their stories, think about how those people are like people you know in your church.

The New Testament also has many letters that people wrote to the churches and to individual people as the church was just getting started. These letters reminded these very first Christians how they were to live together, how they were to treat other people, and how they were to love like Jesus.

What pictures of Jesus and the church do you want to remember? How will those pictures and stories help you remember how Jesus wants you to live in this world?

Beginnings

In this first section of the New Testament stories, you'll read about Jesus' birth. This story has a lot of scenes. First, the angel brought this news to Mary. Mary's cousin Elizabeth, and Elizabeth's husband, Zechariah, also learned that they were going to be parents. Then angels announced Jesus' birth to shepherds. Magi traveled from a great distance to bring him gifts. Simeon and the prophet Anna were very happy about the birth of the One promised by God.

Can you imagine what Jesus' life must have been like between the time when he was ten or twelve and when he grew to be an adult? The Gospel writers don't tell us anything about that time. It's fun to think about what he would have been doing. What do you think his life was like at home with his family? What kinds of things do you think he was doing and learning as a Jewish child when he went to the temple? We have only one story in the New Testament about Jesus as a child. It was the time when he managed to escape from his parents and go to the temple. There Jesus sat with the teachers, listening and asking questions.

The story of his life continues when we meet John, the son of Elizabeth and Zechariah. John was sent by God to prepare the way for Jesus and to baptize him. Rising from the waters of his baptism, Jesus doesn't have much time to pause. The devil makes him stop and think about what things are really important. After taking time alone in the desert to prepare for his work, Jesus is ready. He begins his ministry by calling people. He chooses people he thinks will be willing and able to be disciples, good helpers.

These early stories help us learn about the beginnings of the life of Jesus. As you read these stories, you'll also hear about the people who met him and how their lives changed in so many ways.

How Can This Happen?

Based on Luke 1:26–38

Has someone ever told you something that you didn't understand? Did you feel confused? Did you wonder about why it was said to you? This happened to a woman named Mary.

Mary and Joseph lived in the village of Nazareth. They would soon be married. One day, the angel Gabriel showed up at Mary's house. He said, "Mary, you should be very happy! God has chosen you for something very special. God is with you!"

An angel had never come to her house before. Mary was surprised. The angel said, "It's okay! God sent me with a message for you. You will have a baby boy. You will name him Jesus. He will be king one day. He will sit on David's throne. And his realm will never end!"

Now Mary was surprised and confused. "How can this happen?" she asked. "Joseph and I aren't ready to have children yet."

"This baby will be a gift from God," said Gabriel. "The Holy Spirit will come to you. Your baby will be very special. People will call him God's son. Listen, Mary, your cousin Elizabeth will also have a baby, even though she is very old. God can do anything!"

Mary thought about what the angel said. God was with her. She didn't feel so confused or surprised anymore. She said to the angel, "I will do what God asks me to do."

Then Gabriel, the messenger from God, left Mary. She had a lot to think about!

Hear: Have you ever done something that you had never done before? How did you feel after you did it?

See: Draw a picture of Mary's face while the angel is talking to her. How do you think it changes?

Act: Mary did a brave thing in saying yes to God. What brave thing have you done?

A Prophet Is Born

Based on Luke 1:5–21, 57–80

When a baby is born or adopted by a family, parents wonder how he will grow or what she will do, especially as the baby grows bigger and older. Ask your parents what they thought you would be like. Elizabeth and Zechariah had a good idea what their son would be like.

Elizabeth and her husband, Zechariah, loved each other very much. They wanted to share that love with a baby. They prayed for a baby. But they were very old and had never had a baby.

Zechariah was a priest. One day at the temple, the angel Gabriel showed up. He said, "Zechariah, God is happy with you. You and Elizabeth will have a baby. His name will be John. He will be a prophet filled with the Holy Spirit. He will prepare people for the One God sends."

"But we are too old," said Zechariah.

The angel said, "God sent me to tell you this good news. I promise you it is true. But because you don't believe me, you will not be able to speak until after your son is born."

When Zechariah left the temple, everyone could see that something had happened to him.

Elizabeth and Zechariah did have a baby. Everyone came to see him. "What is his name?" they asked. They thought he would be named after his father.

Elizabeth said, "His name is John."

The people turned to Zechariah, who still couldn't talk. "No one in your family has that name," they said.

Zechariah wrote on a tablet, "His name is John."

At that moment, Zechariah could speak again. He praised God. He told his son, John, "You will grow up to be a prophet of God. God has a special job for you."

Hear: What do you think Zechariah wanted to say while he was waiting for John to be born?

See: What do you think the angel Gabriel looked like?

Act: Have you ever gotten something after you waited for a long time? How did you say thank you?

A Baby Is Born

Based on Luke 2:1–7

What do you know about the day you were born or when you were brought home? Who was there? How did you get your name?

After the angel Gabriel visited Mary to tell her the news about her baby, she and Joseph got some more news. They heard that the Roman ruler, Caesar Augustus, wanted to count all the people in the Roman Empire; every man had to go to his hometown so that his family could be counted. Joseph's family was from Bethlehem. So Mary and Joseph left their home in Nazareth to go to Bethlehem. The trip was hard for a pregnant woman. Just imagine what it would have been like for Mary to make that trip with Joseph!

While Mary and Joseph were in Bethlehem, they looked and looked for a place to stay. It wasn't easy! Many people had come to Bethlehem. Every guestroom was

full. At last, they found space in a room where the animals stayed. The baby was born in that room.

Mary gently wrapped him in cloths and laid him in the manger, where the animals ate. This was the baby that the angel Gabriel had told her she would have.

Hear: If Mary's baby was born in the room where the animals stayed, what sounds do you think he heard?

See: What animals do you think were in the room where Jesus was born?

Act: Mary and Joseph had trouble finding a place to stay. Have you heard about or known people who had no home? What can you do to help these people?

Surprise Visitors

Based on Luke 2:8–20

Have you ever seen a real sheep? Taking care of sheep is hard work. People who take care of sheep are called shepherds. They stay with the sheep all the time and make sure that they are safe.

On the same night Jesus was born, shepherds in a field near Bethlehem saw an amazing sight. They were watching their sheep, as they did every night. Suddenly, an angel stood in front of them. A bright light surrounded them. The shepherds were frightened.

The angel said, "Don't be afraid! I have good news for you! A baby was born tonight in Bethlehem. This baby will be your Savior. He is Christ the Lord! Look for him wrapped in cloths and sleeping in a manger."

Then many angels appeared and said, "Glory to God and peace to all people!"

As quickly as they came, the angels left.

"Let's go find this baby!" said the shepherds.

The shepherds left their sheep and hurried to Bethlehem. They found the baby lying in a manger, just like the angels said. They told Mary about the angels. She was amazed and thought carefully about what they said. She wanted to remember this night forever.

The shepherds went back to their sheep. As they walked, they praised God and told everyone they saw what had happened. What great news!

Hear: Why do you think God chose shepherds to be the first visitors to see Jesus? What do you think Mary wanted to remember about this special night?

See: What colors would make the sky as bright as when the angels appeared?

Act: People love hearing good news. Do you have any good news to tell a friend?

Anna and Simeon

Based on Luke 2:25–38

Sometimes there are things that are very old yet also new. Families take their child to be dedicated or blessed at a church or synagogue. This has been going on a very long time and still goes on today. Ask your parent about your baptism or dedication.

When Jesus was eight days old, Mary and Joseph took him to the temple in Jerusalem. In those days, the oldest son in the family was dedicated to God in the temple.

Simeon lived in Jerusalem. He studied God's word. Simeon wanted so much to see the promised One from God before he died. The Holy Spirit told him, "Simeon, you will get to see the One from God before you die."

On the same day that Mary and Joseph brought Jesus to the temple, the Holy Spirit urged Simeon to go to the temple. Simeon spotted baby Jesus. He knew this baby was the One from God, Israel's new leader. Simeon went to Mary, Joseph, and Jesus. He was so excited! He took Jesus in his arms and praised God. He said, "I have seen the One from God who will be the light for all people."

Mary and Joseph were surprised by Simeon's words. Simeon handed Jesus back to Mary. He said, "This baby will save Israel. But not all people want peace. Since you love Jesus, it will hurt you when they do not listen to him."

The prophet Anna was also in the room. She was very old, and she lived at the temple. She prayed there day and night. Just when Simeon gave Jesus to Mary, Anna praised God and told everyone there about this special baby.

Hear: Have you ever been sad and then something gave you hope? What is hopeful about this story in the temple?

See: If there were other people in the temple that day, what do you think they saw?

Act: It can be hard to wait for a special time of fun or an important thing to happen. How can you wait patiently?

Visitors from the East

Based on Matthew 2:1–12

Imagine getting ready for a long trip, one that would take months. What would you pack? In this story, some people go on a trip that took years. They weren't even sure where they were going.

In a land east of Bethlehem lived some magi. These people studied the stars in the night skies. They looked for new stars, too. One night they saw a new star, a bright star. They believed that this star was a sign that a new king was born. They packed their camels for a long trip to follow the new star.

About two years later, they arrived in Jerusalem. They went to the palace and asked King Herod about the star and the new king. King Herod didn't know anything about a new king or where this baby could be found. He called together the priests and his advisors.

The priests said, "Prophets wrote that a baby king would be born in Bethlehem. He would be king of the Jews. This must be the reason for the star!"

Hearing about a new king did not make King Herod happy. There could be only one king in the land, and *he* was the king. But King Herod was clever. He asked the magi to follow the bright star until they found this new king.

"When you find this new king," said King Herod, "come tell me where he is so that I can honor him too."

The magi followed the star. In Bethlehem, it led them to a house where they found Mary and the child Jesus. The magi knelt before the child. They gave him presents of gold, frankincense, and myrrh.

In a dream, God told the magi not to go back to King Herod in Jerusalem. So they went home a different way.

Hear: Why do you think God chose a star to tell the magi that Jesus was born?

See: What do you think the magi saw when they first met Mary and little Jesus?

Act: What gift would you give Jesus?

When Jesus Was Twelve

Based on Luke 2:39–52

Have you ever wanted to do something all by yourself without any help from an adult? Have you ever been so interested in something that you wandered off by yourself? This happened to Jesus when he was twelve years old.

Jerusalem was crowded with people. They had come to celebrate the Passover festival. During Passover, Jewish people remembered that God freed them from slavery in Egypt many years ago.

Mary, Joseph, and Jesus were in Jerusalem, too. Jesus was twelve years old. They had walked with friends from their home in Nazareth. They traveled with other families so that they would be safe on the road to Jerusalem. Jesus and the other children were excited about their first trip for Passover.

When the festival was over, people from Nazareth began their long walk home. They walked in groups, just as they had come. At the end of the first day of walking, Mary and Joseph didn't see Jesus with his friends. They looked, but he was not with the group of travelers. They hurried back to Jerusalem to look for him.

The worried parents looked everywhere for three whole days. They searched the busy markets. They pushed through the crowded streets. Finally, they found Jesus in the temple, talking with the teachers.

Jesus was asking questions. The teachers were surprised at how well Jesus understood what they said. Jesus was also teaching them. The teachers were listening to all the wonderful things Jesus told them about God.

"Jesus," Mary said, "we've been looking all over for you! We were worried."

"Why were you looking for me?" Jesus asked. "Didn't you know I needed to be in God's house?"

Mary and Joseph didn't understand what Jesus meant. But they didn't question him.

The family left the temple and began the walk to Nazareth. Mary remembered what had happened in Jerusalem, and she thought about that day over and over.

Jesus grew bigger and wiser. God and everyone who knew Jesus were pleased with him.

Hear: Why do you think Jesus stayed in the temple?

See: How do you think Mary and Joseph looked when they found Jesus?

Act: What questions would you have asked the teachers in the temple?

Shhh, Listen!

Based on Luke 3:1–6

Think of a time when you wanted to tell someone something important. How did you know that the person was listening to you?

Listening was important to John, the son of Elizabeth and Zechariah. He was a prophet of God. He listened for God's voice. John went to the desert to listen to God carefully. In the desert, nothing and no one would bother him. He wanted to get ready for the special job God had given him. John was going to help people get ready for Jesus.

When John left the desert, he walked to the Jordan River. God gave him the job of baptizing people there.

John shouted to the people nearby, "Come! Be baptized! Tell God you are sorry for the hurtful things you have said and done. Tell God you want to change your hearts and how you live."

People who knew the prophet Isaiah's words from God remembered:

"A voice will cry in the desert,
'Prepare the way for God!'"

All kinds of people heard John. Day after day, they came to tell God they were sorry. Then John baptized them in the Jordan River. He baptized so many people that he was called John the baptizer.

Hear: What do you think God said to John in the desert?

See: If you were to act out this story, which character would you like to be?

Act: Where do you go to listen to God?

An Awesome Day

Based on Luke 3:21–22

Some people are baptized when they are tiny babies. Others are baptized when they are children, and some are baptized when they are adults. You may or may not have been baptized, and that's okay too! Would you be surprised to learn Jesus was baptized when he was thirty years old?

John, the son of Zechariah and Elizabeth, grew up to be a prophet of God. When he was born, his father had said that he would be a prophet. Now people gathered around John, who was called John the baptizer. He helped people get ready for Jesus. Besides baptizing people, John taught them about sharing and being honest.

John talked about God as if he knew what he was saying. Some people asked him, "Are you the One sent by God?"

"No, no," John said. "I'm here to help you get ready for Jesus, the One God will send."

One day, along with other people, Jesus came to the Jordan River. John was standing in the river baptizing people. When Jesus came to him, he baptized Jesus.

After Jesus was baptized, he prayed to God. Then the heavens opened, and the Holy Spirit came down to Jesus in the shape of a dove.

A voice came from heaven and said, "Jesus, you are my child. I love you very much. You make me happy."

Then Jesus left the river, and John continued to baptize people.

Hear: What do you think God's voice sounds like?

See: Which part of this story do you like most? What colors would you use to draw it?

Act: Baptism is a special gift from God. How can you remember this special gift?

A Wild Test

Based on Luke 4:1–12

It can be very tempting to eat something we aren't supposed to, especially when we are hungry! Sometimes being hungry makes us cranky and tired. Jesus is very hungry in this story.

After Jesus was baptized, he went into the desert wilderness. He went there to spend time with God. For forty days, Jesus walked among the rocks and sand. And Jesus didn't eat a single thing for forty days! He must have been very hungry.

Jesus was not alone. The one who tries to get people to do things they aren't supposed to do, the devil, was there. The devil said, "If you are so hungry, turn that stone next to you into a loaf of bread! You are God's child. Surely you can do that!"

Jesus answered, "Oh no, God's law says people can't live only on bread. We need God, too."

The devil tried again. "Let's go up this hill. I want to show you something."

At the top of the hill, the devil showed Jesus the world as far as they could see. "Jesus, I will give you all these places. They will be yours. You will be rich and powerful, if you worship me."

Jesus answered, "No! God's law says we are to worship God only!"

The devil tried a third time. They went to the temple in Jerusalem. Jesus stood on the very top of the temple. The devil said, "Since you are God's child, go ahead and jump from here. The scriptures say that God will send angels to protect you. You won't even stub your toe!"

Jesus answered, "How can you be so foolish? Don't you know that God's law says that we are not to test God? Enough!"

Jesus wasn't interested in anything the devil had to offer, so the devil decided to leave him alone. Jesus left the desert wilderness. He went to Galilee, where he taught about God in the synagogues. People praised him.

Hear: Why do you think the devil wanted Jesus to listen and do these things?

See: If you were to paint a scene from this story, which part would you choose?

Act: Have you ever wanted to do something you weren't supposed to do? What did you do? What helps you make good choices?

Follow Me!

Based on Matthew 4:18–22

When you wake up in the morning, do you ever wonder what your day is going to be like? Do you think about what you are going to do, and then something surprising happens and everything changes? Life is full of surprises!

A long time ago, Simon (who was also called Peter) and his brother Andrew were having a day just like all their other days. They were fishing. Fishing is hard work, especially on the Sea of Galilee. During the day it can be very, very hot. When the sun floats high up in the sky, its bright rays flash off the water. It's hard to see. So fishing is better in the late afternoon or even at night.

One late afternoon, Jesus was walking beside the Sea of Galilee. He saw Simon Peter and Andrew throwing their fishing nets into the water. Jesus called out to them, "Come! Follow me! I will show you how to fish for people."

Peter and Andrew looked at each other and nodded. Without a single question, they left their nets and followed Jesus.

Not far from them were James and his brother John. They were sitting in a boat, repairing their nets with their father, Zebedee. Sometimes fishing nets get caught on rocks or shells and are torn. You can't catch fish with a net that has big holes in it!

Jesus, Peter, and Andrew slowly walked along the water's edge. When they got closer to James and John, Jesus called out to them, "Come and follow me! I will show you how to fish for people."

James and John quickly stopped what they were doing. Leaving their nets with their father, they hopped out of the boat, waded to shore, and followed Jesus.

Hear: Jesus tells the brothers he will show them how to fish for people. What do you think Jesus means?

See: What do you think Jesus, Peter, and Andrew talked about when they were walking?

Act: What are some ways you can follow Jesus?

Parables

Jesus did a lot of teaching, but it wasn't with books or computers or tablets. You're probably not surprised about that! Because he was Jewish, he had been taught stories from the part of the Bible we call the Old Testament, stories and words that had been passed down for many generations.

After his baptism by John in the Jordan River and after he called people to be his disciples, Jesus began to travel to cities and villages. Wherever he went, he paused. He took time to meet people and to teach them. He remembered all the things he had learned at home and at the temple. He began his teaching by telling stories. He used people and examples from nature in these stories, which we call *parables*.

When we read some of the parables that Jesus told, we get clues about the things that he thought were important. Jesus wanted people to know how to make good decisions. He wanted them to know why it was important to help people. He saw how there were a lot of people who were rich and had a lot of money and things. And he saw many people who were poor, who had very little to live on. He wanted people to look around and see all the different ways people were living. He wanted everyone to learn how to share! And he was very interested in helping people think about how they lived together with their friends, family, and their neighbors.

There's one more thing you need to remember about parables. They invite us to think, to imagine life differently. They ask us to look at our own lives, to think about how we are living in the way that Jesus teaches. Parables help us think about the choices we can make. Parables are not very tidy! Hearing them, we are invited to play with them and ask questions and mess around with the story and think about Jesus' invitation to us.

When you hear these parables, think about the people who heard them from Jesus. What do you think the parables meant to them? What do these parables mean to you today?

The Sower

Based on Luke 8:4–15

Have you ever planted seeds in a garden? Did you notice that some seeds grow well and others struggle? Jesus told a story about that. Let's see what he had to say:

"A farmer went out to sow some seeds. He walked in his field and scattered seeds everywhere. Then he went home and waited for them to grow.

"Some of the seeds fell on the paths. They didn't have a chance. The birds came and ate them up.

"Some seeds fell on rocky ground and started to grow. The sun came out, and the plants dried up and died. They had not put down deep roots.

"Some seeds fell among the weeds and started to grow. But the weeds grew faster and crowded out the farmer's seeds.

"Some seeds fell in the good soil. These seeds put down deep roots. They began to grow tall above the ground. Soon they were strong plants. They grew and grew until they produced lots of grain."

The disciples were puzzled, "What does this story mean?" they asked Jesus.

"The seed is the message of God's love," Jesus explained. "God joyfully plants the seeds of love everywhere. You are like the soil. Sometimes you are like the hard ground. You are not ready to hear about God's love. Don't worry. God still loves you, and God keeps on planting.

"Other times you are like the rocky soil. God's message of love starts growing in you, but life gets hard, and God's love seems far away. Don't worry. God still loves you, and God keeps on planting.

"Sometimes you are like the seeds among the weeds. God's message of love starts growing in you, but worries come along and crowd out God's love. God's love seems to disappear. Don't worry. God still loves you, and God keeps on planting.

"But sometimes you are ready to hear about God's love. The message of love grows deep down inside you. It grows and grows. Other people see God's love in you too. When that happens, God rejoices and keeps on planting."

Hear: Why do you think Jesus told this story?

See: Look out a window or take a walk outdoors. What plants do you see? How are they growing?

Act: How is God's message of love in you? What do you need to keep it growing?

The Good Neighbor

Based on Luke 10:25–37

Do you know your neighbors? They can be people next door, down the street, or across town. Jesus told a story about what it means to be a good neighbor, even to people you don't know. In the time of Jesus, the Samaritans and Jews did not like each other at all. Jesus was a Jew, and one day he told this story about a Samaritan and what happened to him.

Wherever Jesus went, people came to listen to his teaching and to ask questions. One day a lawyer came to Jesus with an important question. "Teacher," he said, "the law says that we must love our neighbor the way we love ourselves."

"That's right," Jesus replied.

"Who is my neighbor?" asked the religious teacher.

Jesus answered the question with a story, "One day a traveler was walking down the road from Jerusalem to Jericho. Suddenly, robbers attacked him and stole all his money. They ran away, leaving him lying in a heap on the side of the road. He was badly hurt and needed help.

"After a while, he heard someone coming. It was a priest. *Thank goodness*, the traveler thought, *I'm saved!*

"But the priest was afraid that robbers would hurt him too. He crossed to the other side of the road, looked the other way, and kept on going.

"Later, the injured man heard someone else coming. This time it was a Levite, also a religious leader. Finally, he thought, *Surely this one will stop and help*.

"But the Levite was also afraid of robbers. He crossed to the other side of the road, looked the other way, and hurried by.

"A third time the injured man heard someone coming. This time it was someone coming from Samaria on the way to Jerusalem. *Oh no*, the traveler thought, *It's someone from Samaria. He will never help me*.

"But the Samaritan man did stop. He bandaged the hurt man and lifted him onto his donkey. He took him to an inn. He gave the innkeeper money to look after the traveler until he was well."

Jesus asked, "Who was a neighbor to the traveler attacked by robbers?"

"The one who was kind to him; the one who stayed with him and helped him," the lawyer replied.

"Go and be that kind of neighbor," said Jesus.

Hear: What does this story teach us about being a neighbor?

See: Choose one of the characters in the story. What do you think that person looked like?

Act: Can you think of someone at your school who is new and might need a friend? How can you be a good neighbor to your classmate?

One Hundred Sheep

Based on Luke 15:3–7

Have you ever lost something and wondered where it was? Did your pet ever disappear, and your whole family searched to bring it home safely? Have you ever lost a friend? If any of these things have happened to you, you can imagine how the shepherd in this story felt.

"One hundred sheep! If just a single one were lost, who would notice? Who counted sheep anyway? The man did. The man had a lot of sheep, one hundred of them. He counted them every day.

"One, two, three, four, five, six, seven, eight, nine, ten; he kept counting: 20, 30, 40, 50, 60, 70, 80, 90, 100. It took time to count, a long time.

"One day the man counted: 10, 20, 30, 40, 50, 60, 70, 80, 90, 91, 92, 93, 94, 95, 96, 97, 98, 99. Then he stopped. There were only 99! He must have made a mistake; he had one hundred sheep, not ninety-nine. He counted again.

"Still there were only ninety-nine. One of his sheep was missing! He was responsible for ALL the sheep, all one hundred of them.

"Immediately the man went to look for the lost sheep. He walked and walked, but he saw nothing. He kept walking. He looked to the left. Nothing.

"He looked to the right. Nothing. He walked, and he listened. Still nothing. Then he heard it, a bleating sound.

"He ran toward the sound. And there she was, the lost sheep. He had found her. She was too tired to follow him home, so he lifted her on his shoulders and carried her.

"He was so happy to have all his sheep together that he invited everyone to celebrate. Some people said, 'What's so wonderful? It was only one sheep. You had ninety-nine others.' The man smiled, 'One sheep makes a difference. Without her something is missing. Now my flock is complete.'"

Hear: Why do you think Jesus told this story?

See: Where do you think the shepherd found the missing sheep?

Act: Have you ever noticed someone at school who sits alone at lunch or doesn't have anyone to play with on the playground? Maybe she or he feels kind of lost like the sheep. What can you do to help that person feel welcome?

Ten Coins

Based on Luke 15:8–10

Here's another story about something that was lost. As you hear it, think about why Jesus told this parable about a woman who lost a small coin.

"Ten drachmas, silver coins. Every day the woman would count them.

"Then one day, she counted. She stopped. She couldn't have made a mistake, but she counted again anyway. Still, she counted only to nine. One drachma was missing. She had lost one of her coins.

"The woman lit a lamp to see more clearly. She looked under chairs and in corners. No coin!

"She looked in cupboards and on shelves. Still no drachma! She took a broom and swept the floor. There were crumbs and dust, but no coin! It was her fault.

"She had lost the coin, and now she must find it. She searched again with the light and the broom.

"Finally, she saw something shining and heard a ping. She looked down and there it was—the missing coin!

"She held the coin in her hand for a few moments. Then she carefully placed it with the other drachmas.

"She was so happy to have all her coins. She invited the women in the town to celebrate. Some people said, 'What is so important? It was only one coin.'

"The woman smiled, 'Just one coin matters. Without it something is missing. Now my coin collection is complete.'"

Hear: What do you think she told the women who came to her house to celebrate?

See: Can you draw a picture of the different scenes in this story using water colors or markers or crayons?

Act: Did you ever lose something? Did you go looking for it? Did you find it? What did you do after you found it?

Two Sons and Their Father

Based on Luke 15:11–32

Did you go to school or church this year and someone you knew wasn't there? Maybe she was sick or had moved away. Jesus told this story about counting people. Who is there? Who is missing?

"A family had two sons. One day, the younger son told his father, 'I'm getting out of here. I want my share of the money you have saved for me.'

"So his father gave half of the money to the younger son and half to the older son. This was a bit different, since children didn't usually get that money until their father died.

"The younger son packed his bags and money and traveled far away. He spent everything having a really good time. Then he was in trouble. The country where he was living didn't have enough food. Now he was out of money *and* food. He looked for a job. Finally, someone hired him to feed pigs. He was so hungry. He would have been glad to eat the pigs' food. But no one noticed. No one shared their food.

"The younger son said to himself, *The people who work for my father have more to eat than I do. I'm always hungry. I'm going home. I'll say to my father, 'I've done a bad thing. I lost everything you gave me. I'm a really bad son. I'll work on your farm if you'll feed me.'*

"He was walking down the road when he saw his father was running to meet him. His father hugged and kissed him. The younger son told his father what he had planned to say. Instead of being angry, his father started planning a party. He told his servants, 'Bring the best of everything for my son: a robe, a ring, and new sandals. Fix a wonderful meal so that we can celebrate. My son was lost but now he has come back.' And the party began.

"The older son was working in the field. He heard the music. Moving closer, he saw the dancing and wondered what was going on. Why a party? He hadn't been invited! A servant told him, 'Your younger brother has come back. Your father is having a party to celebrate.'

"But no one noticed the older son wasn't at the party. No one gave him anything to eat. He stalked off angrily.

"His father saw him. He begged his older son to return. The older son said,

'You're giving a party for my brother who left and lost all the money you gave him. I stayed here with you, working all the time. You never had a party for me.'

"The father said, 'I know you have stayed with me, but we need to celebrate. I thought your younger brother was lost forever, but he's alive. He was lost, but not anymore.'"

Hear: What do you think the older brother would like to say to the younger brother?

See: What's another way this story could have ended?

Act: Count the people who love you. Count the people you love. Who else do you want to add?

The Widow and the Judge

Based on Luke 18:2–5

"I'll get you back." Maybe your brother took the truck you were playing with, so you grabbed one of his toys. Has a classmate been really mean to you at school, so you decided to get even? Jesus told a parable that helps us think about how he wants us to treat others. As you hear it or read it, pay attention to the characters in the story Jesus told. What did they say? What did they do?

"Judges were important people in the life of the city. They helped people settle arguments. One judge who lived there did his job, but he did not respect God. This judge didn't even respect people. This judge cared about only what was important to him.

"A woman lived in this same city. She was called a widow because her husband had died. Someone had treated her unfairly. She went to the judge to get what was hers. Every time he showed up to hear cases, she was there. She was determined to win. So she kept going to see the judge day after day. 'Give me what's mine,' she demanded.

"The judge tried ignoring her, but this didn't work. Then the judge told her, 'No, you are not going to win this case.' But she showed up anyway, demanding, 'Give me what's mine!'

"Finally the judge had enough. He said to himself, *This widow is really bothering me. She won't give up. She is causing me extra work. Every time I appear to hear cases in the village, she is there. Everyone sees her and hears her. I don't respect God or people, but I am tired of her.* So finally the judge gave her what she wanted."

Hear: Why do you think Jesus told this parable to his disciples?

See: What's another way the judge could have acted in this story? What's another way the widow could have acted in this story?

Act: Jesus asks us to treat one another fairly and wants us to get along with one another. How can you do this with someone you disagree with?

Who Was Invited? Who Came?

Based on Luke 14:16–24

Jesus was eating with friends. He saw that people were trying to get the best seats at the table. He wondered about that and told his friends this story. It's another parable. As you hear it, think about what you would have done.

"A man decided to have a nice dinner. When everything was ready, he sent his servant out to tell each guest that the dinner was ready for them.

"At the first house, the person said, 'I can't come. I just bought a farm. I must see it immediately. Please tell the host to excuse me.'

"At the next house, the person said, 'I just bought a new team of oxen for my farm. I haven't seen them yet. I can't come. Please tell the host to excuse me.'

"And a third person said, 'I just got married. I can't come.'

"The servant returned and told the host that no one could come to the dinner. He was upset. What was he going to do? The house was ready. The food was cooked. But none of the guests could come.

"He said to his servant, 'If we can't fill the seats with the guests I invited, then we will fill them with guests that I didn't think about inviting. Look for people who would like a really good meal. Invite anyone you see: the homeless woman; the blind teenager; the man who can't walk, who sits on the corner asking for coins.'

"The servant went out with a new guest list.

"He returned and told the man that all the people had been invited. They were seated at the table. And there was still room for more.

"The host was amazed. He told the servant to go out to the roads and alleys. He said, 'Go to any place where you might find someone who wants a good meal and good people with whom to share it. I want my house to be filled with people who want to be here. The people I invited first are missing a great meal.'"

Hear: Why do you think Jesus told this parable? What did he hope people would learn?

See: Where can you see yourself in this story? Who will you be?

Act: Invite your family to help you serve a meal at a homeless shelter or make and take a meal to someone who is shut-in at home.

Something Big from Something Small

Based on Matthew 13:31–33

God is big. How big? God is too big for us to imagine. Jesus helped people know God by telling stories about the "realm of heaven." The realm of heaven is what it is like when everyone lives in God's ways all the time. Each story gives us a little picture of what this would be like.

The realm of heaven is like a mustard seed. Have you ever watched a caterpillar change into a butterfly? Or maybe you have seen a toy car change into a robot. Jesus compared the realm of heaven to how the mustard seed changes. Jesus said, "A farmer plants the teeny, tiny mustard seed. But from that little speck of a seed grows a tree so big that birds can sit on its branches."

The realm of heaven is like yeast. Pretend that you are in a bakery. Take a deep breath. Smell the freshly baked bread. Eat a slice of the warm bread. Mmm! Isn't it tasty?

Something powerful is hidden in the bread. It is yeast. Yeast makes the bread

dough rise. Jesus told this story about a baker to explain more about the realm of heaven: "A baker mixed yeast into sixty pounds of flour. Thanks to the yeast, the flour changed, or was transformed, into a great lump of dough. The dough was enough to bake bread for at least one hundred people."

These are just two stories about the realm of heaven that Jesus told.

Hear: Sixty pounds of flour is a lot of flour! How much do you weigh? Why do you think Jesus used so much flour in this story about the realm of heaven?

See: Find mustard seeds in the spice aisle in a grocery store. Look how small they are. This tiny seed changes into a tree big enough for birds to sit on its branches. Why do you think Jesus would talk about birds finding shelter from something that began so small?

Act: The people who heard Jesus' story about yeast did not think about the yeast we buy in the grocery story. The yeast they used was more like the starter used to bake sourdough bread. Ask someone to help you find a video on the Internet about making sourdough bread. Try making some and sharing it with a friend.

The Generous Landowner

Based on Matthew 20:1–16

Do you like stories? Jesus told stories with surprises, like this one. The surprises helped people think differently about God and life. Listen for something surprising.

"Life with God is like the landowner who went to the marketplace early in the morning. He was looking for people to work for him. 'Work in my vineyard,' he said, 'I will pay you one coin, the same money anyone would pay you.' These people left to work in the vineyard.

"Around nine o'clock that morning, the landowner went to the marketplace again. He saw people waiting for work. 'Work in my vineyard. I will pay you fairly,' the landowner said. These people went to work in the vineyard.

"At three o'clock that afternoon, the landowner returned to the marketplace. Again, he saw people needing work.

"'Work in my vineyard. I will pay you,' he said. So the people went to work in the vineyard.

"At five o'clock the landowner went out again. What did he see? More people needing work! 'Why aren't you working?' he asked. 'No one has hired us,' they said.

"The landowner told them, 'Work in my vineyard.' So they left to work in the vineyard. When it began to get dark, the landowner told his manager, 'Pay the people who were hired last.'

"The people who were hired at five o'clock lined up. Each of them received one coin. Next, the people hired at three o'clock came to be paid. Each received one coin. The same thing happened for the people hired at nine o'clock that morning. Each received one coin. Finally, the people who were hired early in the morning were paid one coin.

"The workers who were hired first pouted. They complained to the landowner. 'That's not fair! We worked the most but were paid the same amount as everyone else.' The landowner said, 'You agreed to work for one coin. Are you jealous because I am generous?'"

After the story, Jesus said, "So the last will be first, and the first will be last."

Hear: What surprised you in Jesus' story?

See: When you go outside, do you see people who need money? Maybe they are hoping to be hired to work for the day or are asking for spare change. What do you think the landowner would do if he saw these people?

Act: What can you and your family do to help people?

The Pearl

Based on Matthew 13:45–46

What makes you happy? Sometimes people think if they own a lot of things, they will be happy. But Jesus wanted people to think differently. So Jesus told them the story of a man who owned many things:

"There was a merchant who spent his days looking for pearls. He was very good at his job. He selected only the finest pearls to sell. How many pearls had he seen? Hundreds? Maybe even thousands! One day, he saw a pearl that was so different he gasped, 'How amazing!'

"Before him was the most beautiful pearl. But it was very expensive. What did he do? The merchant did something very unusual. He went home. He sold everything he owned. Then he purchased that one pearl. The merchant had nothing else to sell. But he had found this most beautiful pearl."

The merchant had to decide what to keep and what to get rid of. Jesus told this parable because he wanted people to think about what they really need to live as God's people.

Hear: If Jesus were here, what questions would you like to ask him about this parable?

See: Draw a picture of all the items the merchant might have sold to purchase the one pearl.

Act: Ask people to answer this question and collect the answers: What is the thing you want most? What is *your* most beautiful pearl?

People Jesus Met

Some people use their phones for taking pictures more than for calls or texting. They have a photo album of friends and family with them all the time. The women and men you will meet in these stories are a part of Jesus' album. When you meet them, you get a glimpse of the time in which he lived, the people he met, and the invitations he offered them. These stories may sound very odd to you. Remember that they happened in a time and place very different from the one in which you live. As you read them, try to imagine why the Gospel writers chose these stories to tell about people Jesus met.

You can meet these people in several ways. You can begin with hearing or reading the story. Or you can start with the picture, noticing what you see, what the artist chose to show you.

The people Jesus met are all very different. They are young and old, female and male, healthy and sick, poor and wealthy. Sometimes we know their names, and sometimes we don't. They are like people you know and people you may meet.

Mary and Martha were sisters who welcomed Jesus into their home. As Jesus was enjoying a meal at the house of a Jewish leader, a woman came to meet him who had not been invited to the meal. What she did surprised everyone there. Jesus met a Samaritan woman at a well where she came to get water, and her life was changed.

The Gospels tell many stories about Jesus' disciples, but there are also women like Susanna and Joanna who helped Jesus. He could also count on the help of the first apostles, men he called to leave their work as fishermen and follow him. He met a tax collector named Zacchaeus, a man others really didn't like at all. A rich man wanted to follow him, and Jesus told him what he must do. A man with a really bad disease called *leprosy* asked Jesus for help.

Jesus' album tells very interesting stories, don't you think?

Mary and Martha

Based on Luke 10:38–42

Sometimes it is easy to know the right thing to do, and sometimes it is hard. Sometimes the choice is between two *good* things, and it is hard to know which one is better. This is a story about a choice that Jesus' friends Mary and Martha had to make.

One day, Jesus, along with the disciples, went to the home of his very good friends, the sisters Mary and Martha and their brother, Lazarus.

Martha showed Jesus how much she loved him by cooking a wonderful meal for him. She knew Jesus stayed busy taking care of other people, so she liked to take care of him.

Mary showed Jesus how much she loved him by sitting down beside him and listening to him talk about God's love. She couldn't get enough of his stories.

Two sisters with two different ways of showing Jesus their love . . . is one way better than the other? Let's listen to what happened:

"Where is my sister?" Martha grumbled under her breath. "Does she think I have six hands? I can't knead the bread and prepare the fish at the same time!"

The longer Martha worked alone, trying to get everything done by herself, the angrier she became. Ready to explode, she marched up to Jesus and said, "Lord, don't you care that I have to do all the work alone? Make my sister help me!"

Maybe Jesus wasn't as hungry as Martha thought. Or maybe Jesus knew that Mary needed to hear about God's love more than she needed to cook. He said, "Martha, you are running around like crazy! Why are you trying to do so many things? Look at what Mary's doing. What could you learn from her choice?"

Hear: Take a few minutes just to be still and listen. You may hear God's love in a dog's bark, or a bird's song, or in the voice of someone who loves you.

See: When you see a family member working really hard to get everything done, lend a hand. That's a wonderful way to show your love.

Act: When you don't know the right thing to do, listen to your heart. If it's a big challenge, ask a grown-up you trust to help you.

The Thankful Woman

Based on Luke 7:36–48

Feet. Some people think feet are ugly and stinky. Other people think feet are funny and cute. Feet can be ticklish or tough. Many of us depend on our feet to get us where we need to go. At least to get us to our cars or buses or bikes or trains.

In Jesus' day, no one had cars or buses or bikes or trains. Most everyone traveled by foot. In sandals. Imagine how dusty and dirty and sore your feet would be at the end of the day. Now imagine going to someone's house for supper, with everyone seated on the floor around a low table. Would you want someone's dirty feet near your plate? No! In Jesus' day, you washed your feet when you went for a visit.

One day, Jesus was eating at the home of one of the leaders from the synagogue. A woman carrying a jar of perfume came into the room. She seemed happy and sad and scared and excited all at the same time. She walked over to Jesus and began to cry! She couldn't stop crying. She got down on the floor at Jesus' feet and let the tears wash the dirt away. Instead of a towel, she used her long hair to dry his feet. Everyone was watching. Next, she opened the perfume and poured it on his tired, aching feet.

"She's a bad person," someone whispered. "Why is Jesus letting her do this?"

"A bad person?" said Jesus. "You didn't give me water to wash my dirty feet. She washed my feet with her sad, happy tears. You didn't give me a towel to dry my feet. She dried them with her hair. You didn't give me any gifts. She gave me her perfume."

"I don't see a bad person," said Jesus. "I see someone who is sorry for making mistakes. I see someone who loves God very much." Then Jesus turned to the woman and said, "Don't ever forget that God loves you even more."

Hear: Listen to God's voice in Bible stories. People might try to tell you that you aren't good enough, but God will always say to you, "I love you!"

See: Look at your feet. Where did your feet take you today, either by walking or in your wheelchair? Say a prayer of thanksgiving for the places you have been and all the places God will lead you.

Act: Find something that has a wonderful smell. Perfume? A flower? Your favorite food? How does that smell make you feel? How could you share that good smell with someone as a reminder of God's love for them?

The Very Thirsty Woman

Based on John 4:1–32

Turn on a faucet, and watch the fresh water flow. Water to fill a glass or a pet's water dish. Water to fill a pot for cooking rice. It wasn't always that easy. In Jesus' time, the village women carried large buckets from their homes to the well. They filled them and carried them home. Gallons and gallons of water.

Jesus was traveling through a town called Sychar in Samaria. He was thirsty, so he looked for a well. Jesus asked a village woman, "Would you give me a cup of water?"

The woman's mouth dropped open in shock. "You are Jewish. I am a Samaritan. Jews don't like Samaritans. Samaritans don't like Jews." (The Jewish people and the Samaritan people had a serious disagreement long, long ago. They couldn't agree about the correct place to worship God. It caused lots of problems.)

Jesus wanted the world to be different. He wanted to help people forgive one another. He wanted people to learn new ways to live in peace. Jesus said, "I am thirsty for the water in your well. But I think you are thirsty for water from mine. I can give you water that will fill you with life."

The woman had never heard of water like that. She couldn't imagine where Jesus could get it. Jesus told the woman things about herself: "I understand that your life is complicated and hard." Jesus and the woman talked and talked. "I am waiting for God's special one to come," she told Jesus. "He will teach us everything."

"I am God's special one!" said Jesus. The happy woman ran home to tell everyone the good news. "God's special one is here! He will give us the water of life!"

Jesus stayed two more days in Sychar. He made many new friends and told all who wanted to listen about God's generous love.

Hear: Listen to the sound of water as it flows for your bath or from the hose or faucet. Listen to rain. Say a prayer of thanks for fresh water to keep your body healthy. Say a prayer of thanks for the "living water" of God's love.

See: When did you see God's love flowing like fresh water today? Did someone help you today? Forgive you for a hurt? Did you help someone? Forgive someone?

Act: Ask an adult in your life if you could keep water bottles in your car, home, or church to pass out to homeless people or other thirsty people you may see.

Joanna and Susanna Help Jesus

Based on Luke 8:1–3

Jesus' work kept him very busy. When he wasn't telling stories about God's love, he was making someone well. When he wasn't making someone well, he was feeding someone who was hungry. When he wasn't feeding someone who was hungry, he was answering someone's very big questions about God. Jesus loved his work.

Night and day Jesus stayed busy, but he didn't have a "job." Since he didn't have a job, he didn't have any money. He didn't have a house to live in. He didn't have a wallet because he didn't have any money. How did he live? How did he purchase food? Where did he sleep? The answer to these questions? His friends.

Many people saw the wonderful things that Jesus did. The feeding and the praying. The teaching and the healing. They saw these things, and they wanted to help him. Two of these helpers were Joanna and Susanna.

Joanna and Susanna had once been very sick. They had been so sick that no one could make them well. No one except Jesus. He healed them! They felt so grateful to Jesus that they wanted to do something for him. They prayed and they thought and they thought and they prayed. Then they came up with an idea.

They saw that Jesus had no house to live in. They saw that Jesus didn't have a wallet because he didn't have any money of his own. They were worried. "Who takes care of Jesus? What could we do to help him?"

Joanna and Susanna looked at their wonderful houses. They looked inside their full purses. They said, "We have more than we need. We will use our money to feed Jesus and his friends. We will use our money so that he can find a place to stay when he travels."

Joanna and Susanna, and others like Mary and Martha and the disciples, were all part of Jesus' work. Their help made it easier for Jesus to share God's love. Their support reminded Jesus that he was never alone.

Hear: You can find another story about Joanna and Susanna in the Bible. Ask a grown-up to help you find Luke 24:1–12. What wonderful surprise did Joanna and the other women experience?

See: Look for helpers around you. Where do you see people helping at home, school, or church? What could you do to lend a hand?

Act: Joanna and Susanna had money to share, and they worked together to use it to help spread God's love. Start a penny jar and see how long it takes to fill. How could you use this money to help others?

Jesus Chooses Twelve Disciples

Based on Matthew 10:1–4; Mark 3:13–19

Who are your teachers? Think about anyone who helps you learn something new. Teachers also help us figure out problems on our own. After our teachers know that we can solve problems, they give us new things to do. And when we become really good at doing them, we can teach someone else.

Jesus loved to teach. He also knew that many people wanted to hear him teach, and he couldn't do it alone.

One day, he went up on a mountain and asked some people to go with him. He chose twelve men and called them disciples. The disciples were Jesus' students.

Jesus asked Simon to join him and changed his name to Peter. Peter means "rock." He also chose Peter's brother, Andrew. Jesus chose two other brothers, James and John. Their dad was Zebedee, but Jesus called them "Sons of Thunder." Jesus also made disciples of Philip, Bartholomew, Matthew, and Thomas. There was another disciple named James; his dad was Alphaeus. Jesus made Thaddaeus a disciple. He also chose another man named Simon who was from Canaan. Judas was also chosen by Jesus. Sometimes these twelve disciples are called the Twelve.

Some of the men were fishermen. One was a tax collector. But Jesus showed them how to do new things. Jesus taught the Twelve so that they could tell other people about God. When they were ready, Jesus sent them to teach about God and heal people who were sick. The disciples traveled with Jesus until the day he died. With the Twelve, Jesus began his work knowing that he would have help. He had help from God and the disciples.

Hear: Imagine a conversation that the disciples had after they were called by Jesus. What do you think they said? What might they have asked Jesus?

See: When you grow up, what are some things you think you would like to do to be a follower of Jesus? What will you need to learn to do this?

Act: What kinds of things do your parents, teachers, and your church want you to learn? What things can you teach to someone else?

The Short Man

Based on Luke 19:1–10

Have you ever known someone whom nobody liked? Sometimes we don't like people who are different from us, different in how they speak or look or act. Jesus met someone like that.

Jesus was walking, on the way to Jerusalem, with his disciples. To get there, they had to go through Jericho. Zacchaeus was a rich tax collector who lived there. No one in Jericho liked tax collectors. The people who lived there hated Zacchaeus because he worked for the Romans, who had taken over their land. The money they paid Zacchaeus went to the Romans. The tax collectors could take more money than they gave to the Romans and keep it for themselves. That's how they earned their living. But some tax collectors kept a lot for themselves. That's why the people didn't like or trust them.

Zacchaeus heard that Jesus was on the way to Jericho. He wanted to see Jesus, so he went to the road where Jesus was coming. Lots of people were already there. Zacchaeus couldn't see a thing because he was very short. No one would let him through to the front.

Then Zacchaeus had an idea. "I'll climb up into a tree. I'll climb that sycamore tree!"

Jesus got to where Zacchaeus was. He looked up and said, "Zacchaeus, what are you doing up there? Hurry and come down! I would like to come and see you in your house today."

Zacchaeus climbed down from the tree and welcomed Jesus to his home. People saw this and began to whisper to one another. They said, "Look! Jesus has gone to a sinner's house!"

Zacchaeus stopped and said to Jesus, "Lord, I give half of what I own to the poor. And if I cheated anybody out of anything, I will pay them back more than I took."

Jesus said, "Zacchaeus is not a bad person. He understands what I have been teaching. He helps other people. He is a son of Abraham!"

Hear: What would you do if Jesus said that he was coming to your house?

See: Try to imagine Zacchaeus climbing the tree to see Jesus. What would you put in this picture?

Act: Is there someone at school who eats lunch alone? Try sharing your lunch with her or him.

The Thankful Man

Based on Luke 17:11–19

When someone shares a snack with you, what do you say? If your sister is carrying something heavy and you open the door, what might she say? "Thank you," of course. Listen for someone who says "thank you" to Jesus in this story.

Ten men stood by the side of the road. Everyone kept away from them because they were lepers. Lepers were people who had a skin disease like a rash. They couldn't be around other people. So lepers lived by themselves on the edge of town. They stood near the road so that they could call out for help, food, or anything they needed. The ten men wished they did not have the skin disease. They wanted to be able to live with their friends and family.

Jesus and his disciples were on their way to Jerusalem. To get there, they had to pass by the village where the lepers lived. When the lepers saw Jesus, they knew that he could help them. They called out, "Jesus! Please help us!"

Jesus looked at them and said, "Go to the temple and let the priests see your skin." Jesus told them to do this because the priests needed to see that their skin was clean.

The ten men left to go to the temple. While they were on their way, they were healed. One of the men saw that his skin disease was gone. He said, "This is amazing! Now I will be able to live with my friends and family again. I have to go back and thank Jesus!"

This man was a Samaritan. The Samaritans and Jews didn't like each other. But that didn't stop him from thanking Jesus.

The Samaritan went back and found Jesus. He praised him with a very loud voice so that all could hear. Then he bowed down at Jesus' feet to thank him.

Jesus asked, "Were the other nine men healed too? Where are they? Are they coming back?"

Then Jesus said, "Get up and go. Your faith is what healed you."

It didn't matter that Jesus and the leper were from different places. It didn't matter that nobody wanted to be near lepers or Samarians. Jesus did.

Hear: How do you think the ten men knew that Jesus could help them?

See: Why do you think only one of the men came back to thank Jesus?

Act: What are some of the ways you can help someone who is different from you?

The Rich Man

Based on Luke 18:18–30

Have you ever had to do something that was really, really hard? Maybe you had to go somewhere you had never been. Or maybe you had to share something with someone, and you didn't want to do that. This story is about a man who was asked to do something that was very hard to do.

A rich man asked Jesus, "What do I have to do so that I can live forever with God?"

"You know what the commandments are," said Jesus. "Respect those you love. Don't kill people. Don't steal things that don't belong to you. Don't tell lies. Listen to your parents."

"I have obeyed these commandments since I was a little boy," said the man.

But Jesus told him, "There is something else. Go sell everything you have. Give the money to poor people."

The man couldn't believe what Jesus told him. He was sad because he was very rich. This meant he had to give away a lot of things. He knew that would be very hard to do.

Jesus saw that the man was sad. He said, "It's harder for rich people to live forever with God."

People who heard Jesus say this asked him, "If it is hard for rich people, then who can live forever with God?"

"God can do things that humans can't!" said Jesus. "If you give up something for God, you will get things back. Most of all, you will get to live forever with God!"

Sometimes we have to do things that are really hard. Remember that God can help you do anything.

Hear: What would you do if Jesus told you to give all your things to poor people?

See: What are some of the things you think the rich ruler had to give away?

Act: What are some things you need help with? How can you ask God to help you do them?

Healings and Miracles

Sometimes we wonder what is alike and what is different about being a follower of Jesus today. The Bible has a lot of stories about people who were healed or miracles that happened. When you read them, it makes you pause and think. Do these kinds of things still happen today?

All kinds of differently abled people came to Jesus. They wanted to touch him. They wanted his healing presence. Women who were ill, men who couldn't walk, parents who wanted healing for a child who was sick, a man who was blind and wanted to see: they all sought Jesus' healing help. They all came to him believing that with his help, they could be healed. They came with their bodies as they were, and they also came with faith and hope in how Jesus could help them.

There were others who were with Jesus when something happened that we can only call a miracle. There was a large and hungry crowd following Jesus, and all that was in sight was a child who had his lunch—and it was enough to feed everyone. Another time, the disciples were in a boat with Jesus when a terrible storm came up, and Jesus spoke and the waters were calm again, and so were the terrified disciples.

Miracles and healings still happen today, but maybe in ways that are different from the times when Jesus lived. Sometimes sick people are cured. And sometimes they are not. When they are not, we still know God's healing is with us. People help heal our hurt with love and the loving things they do.

When we hear these stories, we remember our faith, our hope, and our prayers for miracles and healing, just like the people Jesus met!

Friends Who Help

Based on Luke 5:17–26

Have you ever had a friend who needed help? What did you do? This story is about four friends who wanted to help their friend who could not walk.

The room was full. No space, not for even one more person. People crowded around Jesus, who sat in the corner, teaching them about God's love. His fellow Jews from Galilee, Judea, and Jerusalem listened carefully.

Up the road came four friends carrying a man on a cot. Their friend could not walk. They knew Jesus could heal him, but they couldn't get into the house. What could they do?

"I have an idea," said one friend. "Let's go up to the roof. We can make a hole and lower him down." Carefully, they climbed the stairs to the roof. They lowered him down in front of Jesus.

Jesus looked up. He saw how much the four friends loved the man on the cot. He told the man who could not walk, "Friend, you are forgiven."

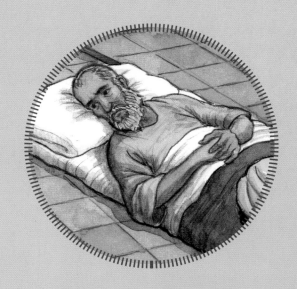

His fellow Jews looked at one another. "Who is this person who thinks that he can forgive other people? Only God can forgive."

Jesus knew why they were saying this. He said to them, "What's your problem? Is it easier to say, 'You are forgiven' or to say, 'Stand up and walk?' Pay attention so that you can understand that God has given me the power to heal and forgive sins."

Jesus said to the man who could not walk, "Stand up. Pick up your cot, and walk home."

Immediately, the man stood up. He picked up his cot and walked out of the house. As he left, he praised God.

The people in the crowded room were amazed by what they had seen. They praised God, too. Many said, "We have seen many incredible things today."

Hear: Why did people come to hear and see Jesus?

See: God wants us to help and love other people. How were the four friends helping the man who could not walk? How was Jesus loving and helping all those in the crowd?

Act: When have you seen people helping and loving others? What were they doing? How do you help and love others?

Jesus Heals a Woman and a Girl

Based on Luke 8:40–56

Do you know someone who has been sick for a long time? What can you do to help?

A crowd waited on the shore of the Sea of Galilee for Jesus to get there. Some people were sick. Others were just curious. A religious leader, Jairus, was in the crowd. As soon as Jairus could get to Jesus, he fell at Jesus' feet. "Teacher," he asked, "will you come to my house? My twelve-year-old daughter is very sick."

In the same crowd, a woman who had been sick for twelve years tried to get close to Jesus. She had spent all her money on doctors. Nothing worked. Jesus was her last hope.

If I can just touch Jesus, I will be healed, she said to herself. *But he is so far away.*

She pushed and gently shoved. When she was close enough, she touched Jesus' clothes. She knew she was better right away.

Jesus turned and asked, "Who touched me?"

"Not I, not I," said the people close to him.

"The crowd is so big," said Peter. "Everyone is pushing you."

But Jesus knew someone touched him.

The woman fell at Jesus' feet. "I touched you, and I was healed right away!" she said.

"You were healed because you believe," Jesus said. "Go and be happy!"

A man who worked at Jairus's house came to them. "Jairus," he said, "your daughter died. Don't bother Jesus anymore."

Jesus heard what the man said. He told Jairus, "Don't be afraid. Trust in me, and she will live."

Everyone was crying at Jairus's house. Jesus said, "Don't cry. The girl is just asleep." People laughed at him. They knew the girl was not alive.

Jesus went to the girl and gently took her hand. He said, "Little girl, wake up."

The girl woke and stood up.

"Get her something to eat," Jesus said to the parents.

"Our daughter is alive. Alleluia," they shouted.

"Do not tell anyone that I healed your daughter," Jesus ordered the girl's parents.

Hear: I wonder why the sick woman was afraid to tell Jesus that she had touched him. Why do you think she finally decided to tell Jesus that it was her?

See: Close your eyes and imagine what the big crowd around Jesus looked like. Who do you think was there besides the woman who had been sick for twelve years and Jairus? Why do you think they came to see Jesus?

Act: You may not be able to heal people like Jesus did, but you can help them feel better. What might you do for someone in your family who doesn't feel well?

Jesus Heals with Words

Based on John 4:46–54

What it would be like without telephones or computers that we can use to talk with people far away? Without telephones and computers, people still heard about Jesus and how he healed people. In this story, Jesus does not need to see or touch someone to make them well.

In Capernaum, an important royal official was worried. His son was very sick. He heard that Jesus could make sick people well. When he heard that Jesus was headed to Capernaum, this important official began the long walk to meet Jesus. The journey was long, hot, and dusty. The official walked more than a day before he saw Jesus.

When the official reached Jesus, he fell to his knees. He begged Jesus, "My son is very sick. Please come to my house."

"You just want to see a miracle," Jesus said.

"I want you to make my son better. Please come."

But Jesus said, "Go back home. Your son is alive."

The official trusted Jesus. He started the long journey home.

Before he arrived at his house, his servant ran to meet him. "Your son is alive and well."

"When did he get better?" asked the boy's father.

"Yesterday at one o'clock in the afternoon."

"That is the same time I was talking with Jesus. Jesus healed my son without seeing or touching him. Jesus is amazing!"

After this, the official and everyone in his house trusted in Jesus.

Hear: How do you think the boy's father heard about Jesus if there were no telephones or computers?

See: Pretend you are the royal official. Act out the story without using words. How would you look as you walked to meet Jesus? How would you look when your servant came to meet you?

Act: If someone is sad or sick, how can you help them if you cannot see them or be with them?

Jesus Heals a Woman on the Sabbath

Based on Luke 13:10–17

The Sabbath is a day of rest for the Jewish people. In the time of Jesus, there were many customs about honoring the Sabbath as a day of rest. Rules about both what one could do and what one what one could not do to honor the Sabbath. In this story, Jesus raised a question about healing on the Sabbath.

Jesus was teaching in the synagogue on the Sabbath. A woman was there in the crowd. She could not stand up straight because her back was so bent over. She had been like this for eighteen years. Jesus saw her and said, "Woman, you are free." Then he put his hands on her, and slowly, very slowly she was able to stand up straight. Finally she was able to see faces, not feet. She saw Jesus. "I am healed," she said. "Hurrah, God!"

The leader of the synagogue was not pleased. He rushed over to Jesus. "You should not have healed her on the Sabbath. Today is the day we rest." He was very angry that Jesus had broken this Sabbath rule. He wanted the crowd gathered in

the synagogue to hear him and agree with him. "You can work six days a week, but no one should do any work on the Sabbath. And that includes healing!"

But Jesus said, "Do you feed your animals on the Sabbath? Do you take them to get clean water to drink? Animals need food and water every day. This woman has been walking bent over for eighteen years. She needed to be healed."

After Jesus spoke, the leader and the crowd felt terrible. They knew Jesus was right. The crowd was happy because Jesus was doing many wonderful things for people.

Hear: What rules do you have in your school or in your family? Why do you think you have these rules?

See: What do you think the woman was able to see when she was bent over? Try drawing that picture. What do you think she was able to see after Jesus healed her? Draw that picture.

Act: Helping someone, listening to someone, inviting a child who is all alone at lunch or on the playground to sit or play with you—these are all acts of healing. What healing act can you do?

Jesus Touches People

Based on Mark 8:22–26

Jesus was amazing! Sometimes he would speak and incredible things would happen. Sometimes people needed to be touched by Jesus to be healed. In this story, Jesus touched a man two times before the man was better.

Jesus and his disciples traveled into the town of Bethsaida. People brought a man to Jesus who could not see. They begged Jesus to touch him.

Jesus took the man's hand and led him out of the town. When they were alone, Jesus put his own spit on the man's eyes and touched him. "Can you see anything?" Jesus asked the man.

"Yes," the man answered. "I see people. But they don't really look like people. They look more like trees that are walking."

Jesus put his hands on the man's eyes again. Jesus looked right into his eyes. Suddenly, the man could see perfectly.

"I can see!" said the man. "Jesus healed me!"

But Jesus sent him home saying, "Do not go back into the town."

Hear: Why do you think Jesus had to touch the man's eyes two times before he was better?

See: If you could not see, what do you think it would be like to be able to see suddenly? How would you feel? What would you do?

Act: The man was healed by Jesus' touch. Who do you know who would feel better by a gentle touch from your hand?

A Canaanite Woman Does Not Give Up

Based on Matthew 15:21–28

Have you ever wanted something so badly that you did not give up? In this story, a Canaanite woman, whose name we don't know, was determined that Jesus could make her daughter well. And she did not give up until Jesus helped her.

Jesus left Galilee and traveled with his friends to Canaan. He hoped to get some rest. But people found him there, too, and needed his help.

A woman shouted at Jesus, "Lord, listen to me! Something terrible is happening to my daughter. She is very sick. You can make her better."

Jesus did not say anything.

Jesus' friends said, "That woman is so loud. She is really bothering us. Get rid of her."

But Jesus did not send her away. He said to the woman, "I was sent to help the Israelite people. They are like lost sheep."

The woman was not an Israelite. Yet, she would not leave. She got down on her knees before Jesus. "Lord, please help my daughter," she begged.

"It is not right for me to help you," Jesus said. "I cannot give the food of children to dogs."

The woman cried, "Dogs need food, too. They eat the crumbs that fall from the people's table."

Jesus was amazed that the Canaanite woman trusted him. "You did not give up when I said no! You can have what you wish!"

At that moment, the woman's daughter was made well. The mother did not give up!

Hear: Why do you think Jesus did not help the woman at first? What made him change his mind?

See: The Canaanite woman and her daughter were different from Jesus. Do you think these differences matter to God? Why or why not?

Act: The Canaanite woman's daughter was important to her. Who or what is important to you? What do you do to take care of those people or things that are important to you?

Jesus at the Pool

Based on John 5:1–13

Jesus heard of a wonderful pool,
Airy and shaded and nice and cool.
If you were sick or body broken
This was water you wanted to soak in.

What's that, you ask? How does it occur?
An angel comes and gives it a stir.
The pool can cure the injured and sick.
Could you believe it? Is this a trick?

Jesus was curious, just like you.
Off he went, to see if it's true.
He found people—sick, wounded, blind—
Had come to leave all their pain behind.

One man was behind the first in line,
Even though he'd been there a long time.
Others rushed past with their heads
    bent down,
And no one saw him on the ground.

It didn't take Jesus long to decide
To go to the man, and sit beside,
Look him in the eye, and speak at last:
"Would you like to be well?" Jesus asked.

Then the man told his story out loud:
"I've no one to help me in this crowd.
When I walk to the water, you see,
Someone else steps up in front of me."

Jesus didn't fill the silence with talk,
Just said, "Stand up, take your mat, and
    walk."
Then the man felt entirely whole,
Both in his body and in his soul.

He stood right up from where Jesus
    kneeled.
For in that moment the man was healed.
Others stopped and asked, "Who made
    you well?"
The man shook his head and could
    never tell.

For Jesus had not told him his name,
Yet with love, healed the man all the same.
The man looked left, and the man
    looked right.
But Jesus was nowhere, not in sight.

Hear: What do you think the man heard as he sat by the pool?

See: Have you ever seen someone sitting all alone? Did they look happy or sad? How could you tell?

Act: When have you felt sick or sad? Who helped to heal you?

A Boy and His Lunch

Based on John 6:1–15

Word had spread all across the lands
Of Jesus and his loving hands.
He cured the sick, he healed the blind.
To friends and strangers, he was kind.

The people gathered one by one
To see the things Jesus had done.
To every place that he would go,
The people followed, high and low.

He crossed the Sea of Galilee,
Went up a mountain, through the trees,
Then Jesus came to sit and rest
Among the friends he knew the best.

But even all the way up here,
The crowd had followed, oh so near,
To listen to the words he'd say,
To watch him heal, to hear him pray.

When he saw the large gathered crowd,
Jesus asked this question aloud:
"They've walked for miles on their feet.
Where can we buy them bread to eat?"

He said this with a little smile,
For Jesus planned it all the while,
Just exactly what he would do,
But wondered if his friends knew, too.

Now Philip, who was close at hand,
Did not know what Jesus planned.
For this was not a crowd of tens.
It was five thousand citizens!

"To earn the money we would need
To buy the bread enough to feed
All these people gathered here
Would take us more than half a year!"

Andrew spoke up then and said,
"Here is a boy who has some bread:
Five loaves, two fish—it's all good stuff!
But surely this is not enough."

Jesus took the loaves and then said,
"God, we thank you for all this bread."
He passed the loaves, he passed the fish,
He told the crowd, "Take all you wish."

They all sat down on the ground.
Is there enough to go around?
Five thousand people sitting there,
Somehow they had enough to share.

Once everyone was satisfied,
Jesus walked through the crowd and cried,
"So that not one crumb may be lost,
Gather up what you would have tossed."

The scraps from five small barley loaves
Now made twelve baskets overflow.
What wasn't enough for them before
Had somehow turned into so much more!

When people saw what he had done,
They shouted, "Surely he's the one!
Jesus is the prophet, he who
Has come to make all things anew!"

Jesus didn't want attention.
He realized their intention:
To force him to become their king,
Who would rule all and everything.

Instead of sitting on a throne,
Jesus chose to be all alone.
He did not boast, he did not speak,
Alone he climbed the mountain's peak.

Hear: Imagine sharing a meal with many
friends. What sort of noises would you hear?
What do we say when we pass the food
around the table?

See: Imagine having one loaf of bread.
Suddenly there are five loaves. Then there
are ten loaves! What would it look like to see
more and more food appear? How would
you feel?

Act: When are times when you like to be
alone? When are times when you like to be
with lots of other people?

Calming the Storm

Based on Luke 8:22–25

One day the sun was bright and hot,
And Jesus had a lovely thought:
"Let's pile into a little boat,
And have ourselves a little float.
Across the lake upon the tide,
We'll dock on the other side."

The boat rocked gently in the breeze,
Side to side it swayed with ease.
The water was so calm and deep.
The waves rocked Jesus right to sleep.

The wind picked up across the lake.
The boat began to creak and shake.
Rain poured down, and waves grew tall,
But Jesus slept right through it all!

The group of friends was terrified
As water filled the boat inside.
Around their feet, now it's double!
Without a doubt, they're in trouble.

The storm raged on upon the lake.
They shook their friend Jesus awake.
"Master, master!" they were crying,
"Help us! We are surely dying!"

Jesus knew just what he would do:
He gave those winds a talking-to.
He wagged his finger, shook his head,
And told that storm to go to bed.

The wind stopped howling, just like that.
The waves died down in seconds flat.
The sun came out. The rain was gone.
Once again the water was calm.

Amazed by what they'd seen and heard,
The disciples couldn't say a word.
"Who is this man within our boat,
Who keeps our tiny ship afloat,
Who tells a storm to go away,
And skies and clouds and rains obey?"

Hear: What are some of the sounds you hear outside on a nice day? What are some of the sounds you hear during a storm?

See: Imagine a little boat in the middle of a big storm. How would it be moving? What would it be like to be sitting in that boat?

Act: Think of the things that make you feel afraid. Who do you go to when you are feeling scared? What do they do to calm you?

Endings and Beginnings

Jesus began his ministry by taking some time in the desert; then he left the silence of the desert. In the last days of his life on the earth, Jesus was getting ready to enter the city of Jerusalem. In this section, you will read stories about the events of Holy Week—Palm Sunday and the Passover meal with the disciples in the upper room. You'll hear a story about the trial and death of Jesus. This is a very sad story.

But then there is a really happy story. Women were the first ones to arrive at the tomb where Jesus had been taken. They discovered that his body was not there. And there were other people like Mary Magdalene, Thomas, Peter, and the disciples walking on the road to Emmaus. Each of them has a story to tell about meeting Jesus after his resurrection.

These stories are about endings and beginnings. They remind us about the way that Jesus' life on earth ended. These stories also tell us about the beginnings of new life and hope. As Jesus returned to life and appeared to his friends, they weren't sad anymore. His friends came to know that their lives, like Jesus' life, were beginning in many new ways.

Jesus Visits Jerusalem

Based on Luke 19:29–40

What kind of trips do you like to take with your family or friends? Have you gone on trips in your city or town or farther away? Did you go on a plane, on a train, in a bus, or by car?

Jesus traveled to cities and small towns to teach the people about God's love. One of the most important trips he took was to Jerusalem, the special Holy City.

While he was there, Jesus gave two of the disciples a special task. He said to them, "Go into the village. There you will find a young donkey that no one has ever ridden. Untie it and bring it to me. I want to ride it into Jerusalem."

The disciples were surprised Jesus wanted a donkey to ride, because he always walked everywhere he went. But they loved Jesus and knew he was an important teacher, so they did what he asked. Jesus told them that if anyone asked why they were taking the donkey, they should tell them that he needed it.

They went into the village and found the donkey, just like Jesus had told them. They brought the donkey back to Jesus. The disciples laid cloths on its back so that Jesus could ride it.

Now Jesus was ready to ride into Jerusalem. The people following him began to cheer. Crowds lined the streets. Some people joined the disciples and spread their cloaks on the road to welcome Jesus. Others wondered why everyone was so excited about a man entering the city on a donkey. Powerful rulers rode big war horses.

The disciples praised Jesus, singing and shouting for joy because of God's love for them. The people welcomed Jesus with blessings, saying "Peace!" The people who knew Jesus and his teachings about love and peace were excited that he was in Jerusalem. They expected great things from this teacher from Galilee.

Some teachers of the law (called the Pharisees) were in the crowd. They did not like Jesus being praised so much when he was not a king. They also worried that Jesus would upset the Roman officials. They thought he didn't deserve all this celebration because he was only a teacher riding a donkey. They said to Jesus, "Teacher Jesus, tell your disciples to stop praising you like a king! It's not the right thing to do because you're not our king!"

Jesus told them, "I tell you the truth, if they were silent and did not sing praises, the very stones on this earth beneath us would shout out."

Hear: When have you heard people cheer or shout with joy?

See: Who is in the crowd watching Jesus? Draw a picture of Jesus' followers.

Act: Think of someone you want to celebrate and praise. How would you show that person that you love him or her?

A Passover Meal

Based on Luke 22:1–20

When people celebrate holidays, they often eat special meals together. What kinds of food do you eat at Christmas? At Easter? On your birthday? Jesus and the disciples ate a meal to celebrate the Passover when they were in Jerusalem.

When Jesus and the disciples went into Jerusalem on the day we call Palm Sunday, it was time for the Passover festival. Jewish people traveled from all over to Jerusalem. They came to remember how God sent Moses to lead them out of slavery into the Promised Land. An important part of this celebration was the Passover meal.

Jesus sent his friends Peter and John into the city. He said, "Find a place where we can eat the Passover meal together."

"Where do you want us to prepare the meal? We don't live here," they asked.

"You will meet a man carrying a jar of water," answered Jesus. "He will show you an upstairs guestroom in his house."

Peter and John went to Jerusalem. They saw the man with the water jar. He showed them his upstairs guestroom where the meal could be prepared, just like Jesus had said.

Later, Jesus and all the disciples came to the upstairs room. When the meal was ready, they gathered around the table to eat the Passover meal of lamb, vegetables, and herbs. Jesus looked around the table. He said, "I am glad to eat this Passover meal with you. It might be a long time until we eat together again."

Jesus picked up a cup. He said, "Thank you, God, for this food."

Then Jesus picked up a loaf of bread and tore it into pieces. He gave the bread to his disciples. "This bread is like my body," he said. "Remember me when you eat bread with your friends and family."

When everyone had eaten, Jesus lifted the cup again. He said, "This cup is like the blood that makes each human live. Remember me when you drink from this cup."

This was a new way to celebrate the Passover. The disciples were confused about some things that Jesus said. But tonight, they were happy to be together.

Hear: What do you think Jesus meant when he said, "Remember me?"

See: If you could take a picture of the scenes in this story, what would you show?

Act: Jews share the Passover meal to remember how God set them free from slavery. Christians share bread and cup at Communion to remember Jesus. What else can you do to remember Jesus?

Jesus Dies

Based on Luke 23:1–49

Have you ever been having a good time, and then something bad or sad happens? This is what happened to Jesus after the Passover meal he shared with the disciples. If this part of the story makes you feel sad or scared, read it with a friend or family member.

Some temple leaders didn't like the way so many people listened to Jesus' teachings. They worried that people might not listen to them. So that night, they came to the garden where Jesus was praying. Judas, one of the disciples, pointed them to Jesus. The temple guards grabbed Jesus and arrested him. They took him to the temple leaders. "If you are the one God has sent, tell us," the temple leaders said.

"If I answer, you won't believe me," said Jesus.

"Are you God's son?" they asked.

"You say that I am," answered Jesus.

They took Jesus to Pilate, who was the Roman leader in Jerusalem.

"Are you the 'King of the Jews'?" Pilate asked.

"If you say I am," Jesus answered.

Pilate knew that the Roman king didn't want another king in the land.

Pilate didn't think Jesus had done anything wrong, but some of the temple leaders said he had. Pilate decided to let the people decide if Jesus should die. So Pilate had Jesus and a murderer named Barabbas brought before a crowd of people.

"Which one should I set free?" Pilate asked.

Some people shouted, "Barabbas! Let Barabbas go free!"

"If that's what you want," said Pilate.

The soldiers led Jesus to the top of a hill and placed him on a cross to die. A crowd followed, but only a few women who followed Jesus stood close to him.

About noon, the sky became very dark, like night without stars. Then Jesus died. His disciples and followers were sad. How could they live without Jesus?

Hear: When you are sad or scared, what do people say to comfort you?

See: If you had been in the crowd, what would you have seen and heard?

Act: Write a note or draw a picture for someone who is sad.

Women at the Tomb

Based on Luke 24:1–12

Dying is a part of the life cycle. Think about a plant, any plant, which begins as a seed. First is birth, the sprouting of a seed. Next is growth, the unfurling of stem and leaves. The plant lives and soaks up sunshine and rainwater. Then the plant dries up and dies. But the life cycle, the story of the plant, is not over! New seeds grow in what's left from the old plant. The story was not over for Jesus when he died either.

Jesus had been dead for more than a day. Early on the morning of the third day, Mary Magdalene, Joanna, Mary, the mother of James, and other women who loved Jesus went to the tomb where he had been taken. They walked sadly and quietly, carrying sweet-smelling spices to place on his body.

When they got to the tomb, they were surprised! The stone was rolled away from the cave opening. They looked in, but Jesus was not there. The women were confused and scared. Who had moved the body?

Suddenly, two men in shiny white clothes stood next to them. Afraid, the women turned away.

The men said, "This is where the dead are kept. Jesus is not here. He has been raised to life! Remember what he said when you were with him in Galilee? He said that the One sent from God will be taken by those who don't believe in him. This One will be killed. But on the third day, this One from God will rise to life again."

The women remembered that Jesus had told them these things. They ran back to the disciples, eager to tell them the good news!

"Jesus is alive!" shouted the women. But the disciples didn't believe Mary of Magdala. They didn't believe Joanna. They didn't believe Mary, the mother of James. They didn't believe any of the women.

But Peter wasn't sure. He ran to the tomb. When he got there, he looked inside. This time, the two men in shining white clothes were not there. Peter saw only the cloth that had covered Jesus, but no body. He walked away, wondering if it could be true. Was Jesus really alive?

Hear: The women were excited to share the good news about Jesus. How do you sound when you are excited? Do you laugh or sing or shout?

See: The women left the empty tomb filled with joy. Create art with colors that mean joy to you.

Act: Why is finding an empty tomb good news about Jesus? Tell someone you love the good news!

Thomas Wants to See

Based on John 20:19–31

Have you ever wondered if something you were told is true? Asking questions helps you find answers. Asking questions about Jesus and Bible stories helps you be a better follower of Jesus. Listen for Thomas's question.

On the same day that the women found the empty tomb, Jesus surprised the disciples. They, except for Thomas, were in a room with the door locked. They were afraid that the people who had killed Jesus would look for them.

Suddenly, Jesus was in the room with them, but no one had unlocked the door. "Peace be with you," said Jesus.

Before he left, he showed them the scars on his hands and in his side. The disciples were joyful and happy.

When Thomas came back, they all talked at once: "Jesus is back! We've seen him up close." But Thomas wasn't so sure they were telling the truth. "I'm not sure that I believe what you say. I'll believe you when I see Jesus in person myself. I want to see him with my own eyes."

Eight days later, the disciples were gathered together in the same room. This time Thomas was there too. Suddenly, Jesus was in the room, even though the door was locked. Jesus blessed them, saying, "Peace be with you."

Jesus said to Thomas, "Put your hands on my hands. See the marks where the soldiers hurt me? Here I am, scars and all! Believe that I am alive!"

Amazed, Thomas touched Jesus' scars. He said, "My Lord Jesus! It is you!"

"Thomas," Jesus said, "do you believe it is me because you can see me? Blessed are people who don't see me and still believe that I love them."

After that day, Jesus did many wonderful things. He showed everyone God's love for the world. Some people wrote down what they remembered about Jesus and his stories. Because they did, we can learn more about him even though we can't see him.

Hear: What do you say when you are amazed? Do you shout or sing or pray?

See: If you could see Jesus, like Thomas did, what would you want to ask him?

Act: What is something you wonder about? Make a list of questions. Then ask people you love to help you find answers!

Memory and Surprise

Based on Luke 24:13–35

How do you recognize a friend? By hair color, clothes, or voice? We have many ways to remember people who are important to us. In this story, Jesus' friends recognize him when he does something.

Cleopas and his friend had gone to Jerusalem with Jesus. Now they were leaving. Jesus was dead, and they were going home. They were walking on the road to Emmaus, talking about all that had happened. A stranger caught up with

them and asked, "What are you talking about?"

"You're coming from Jerusalem. Don't you know what happened there?" they said. "Haven't you heard the news about the prophet killed in Jerusalem?"

"What news?" the stranger asked.

Cleopas explained, "Jesus was our friend. He talked about loving others. He was God's prophet. Many people followed him. We thought he would be the one to save us from Roman rulers. But some leaders in the government thought he was dangerous. They killed him three days ago. Today women went to his tomb. They said the tomb was empty! They saw angels who said that Jesus is alive. Now we don't know what to believe. We are sad and confused."

"I know you're sad. Listen to me," said the stranger. "Do you remember what the prophets wrote about the One sent from God?" Then he told them some old stories about the One whom God promised to send. This One would show them how to live together peacefully.

They continued walking together. As the sun set, they arrived in Emmaus. The stranger kept on walking.

"Wait! It's almost night time," said the two disciples. "Please stay with us."

The stranger agreed. When the food was ready, the stranger took the bread. He broke the bread into pieces and gave it to them. Then Cleopas and his friend saw it was Jesus who was sitting at the table with them!

Then Jesus disappeared.

Cleopas said, "It was Jesus who walked with us when we were sad! I felt my heart shine inside me when he told us the old stories."

They were so surprised that they didn't finish eating. They left Emmaus and hurried back to Jerusalem. There the disciples were talking about Peter having seen Jesus. Cleopas and his friend told the disciples what had happened to them. "Jesus is alive! We knew it was him when he gave us the bread."

Hear: The two disciples didn't recognize Jesus when he told them stories from the prophets. What changed so that the two disciples could recognize Jesus?

See: When we are hurrying, sometimes we look right past things in front of us. Take a walk around your home and look closely at everything in it. Which things are most important to you?

Act: Invite a friend for a snack. Tell your friend the story of Cleopas and his friend and how they recognized Jesus when he shared the bread with them.

Mary Finds Her Friend

Based on John 20:11–18

What do you do when you miss someone? Do you remember how you played with the person? Do you like to go to places you went together? Listen for what Mary of Magdala did when she missed Jesus.

Mary of Magdala missed her friend Jesus after he died. She knew the tomb where his body was buried was empty. But she felt close to him there. She stood outside the tomb and cried.

When she looked into the tomb, it wasn't empty. Two angels dressed all in white were there. They said, "Why are you crying?"

"Someone took away the Good Teacher. I don't know where he is!" said Mary.

When she turned around, she saw a man she thought was a gardener.

"Woman, why are you so sad?" he asked. "What are you doing here?"

"Please tell me where Jesus' body is. Did you move him? Please tell me where. I will go get him," Mary said.

The man said, "Mary."

Then Mary knew the man was not a gardener. The man was Jesus. She cried out, "Teacher! You're alive!"

Mary was so excited to see Jesus alive! She wanted to hug him. But Jesus said, "Please don't touch me. Go tell my friends and followers that I am alive. I will soon go to be with God."

Mary was so glad Jesus was alive. She ran to find the other disciples so that she could tell them the good news.

Hear: Mary knew it was Jesus when he said her name. Who says your name in a special way?

See: If you could illustrate this story with chalk or clay or torn paper collage, what scene would you like to show?

Act: Names are important. Make a list of names of people you love. Ask some of them how they got their names or what their names mean. How did you get your name? What does it mean?

Jesus Gives Peter a Job

Based on John 21:15–19

Have you ever been given a difficult job? Were you afraid you wouldn't be able to do it? In this story, Jesus gives Peter a hard job to do, but it is important work for God.

After Jesus came back to life on Easter, he liked to spend time with his friends. One morning, after he made them breakfast on the lakeshore, Jesus asked, "Peter, do you love me?"

Peter was surprised at Jesus' question because he had been with Jesus from the beginning.

"Yes, Jesus, I love you!" said Peter.

"Feed my sheep, the people I love," Jesus said to Peter.

Then Jesus asked a second time, "Peter, do you love me?"

"Yes, Jesus, I love you very much!" Peter answered.

Jesus told him again, "Take care of my sheep, the people I love."

Then Jesus asked a third time, "Peter, do you love me?"

Now Peter was really wondering if Jesus had heard his answer. And he said, "My teacher, you know all about me. You know that I love you and trust you."

"Feed my sheep, the people I love," said Jesus.

Hear: Who says "I love you" to you?

See: What kind of job did Jesus give Peter? What kinds of things can you see him doing?

Act: Peter and his friends followed Jesus. Jesus asked Peter to continue caring for others. Name three ways you can be a follower of Jesus every day.

The Early Church

The Gospels tell us stories about Jesus and the people he met. Now we are moving on to another part of the New Testament. Here we learn about the beginnings of the church. The book of Acts was written by the same person who wrote the Gospel of Luke. It's really like a small history book. In Acts, we read about how the church began. Many of the books in the New Testament after Acts are letters. They are written by Paul and other apostles to the churches in many different places. These books add more pictures to the album. They help us see what life was like for the first Christians after Jesus was no longer living among them.

We begin with hearing about the church celebration we call Pentecost. On this special day after Easter, we remember how God sent the Holy Spirit to the early church. We learn about how this first group of Christians learned how to live in the ways that Jesus had taught them. One of the first things they did was to choose leaders and care for the needs of everyone.

You will also hear stories about particular people who were really important as the church began. As you read about Philip, Lydia, Paul, Silas, and Timothy, you learn about people God called to help with the church. They told others about God's word and God's love.

Pentecost

Based on Acts 2:1–41

What do you feel like when someone you love goes away? Maybe the disciples felt that way after Jesus went to be with God. After Easter, when Jesus came back, he told the disciples to wait in Jerusalem for the gift of the Holy Spirit. So this story begins in Jerusalem.

The disciples waited together. Fifty days, and they were still waiting in Jerusalem. This day was Pentecost, which was a Jewish festival. On this day, Jews remembered how God gave the Ten Commandments to Moses on Mount Sinai. The city was filled with visitors from many lands. The disciples were waiting together in a house. Suddenly, the wind whooshed around them! It howled into every corner. With a great flash, little flames of fire danced over each person's head. But no one was burned.

The Holy Spirit was in that house. The Holy Spirit helped them speak languages they didn't know before.

The noise of everyone speaking carried beyond the walls. People on the street heard the disciples speaking in their languages. "How is this happening?" they asked each other. "Those people are from Galilee. How did they learn my language?"

It was such a strange thing that some people said, "They must be drunk."

Peter said, "We're not drunk. We're full of the Holy Spirit!" Then the Holy Spirit helped Peter tell them all about Jesus. He told them how the prophets prepared everyone for the coming of Jesus. He told the people about God's love for them. He told them that Jesus was killed. He also told them that Jesus came back from the dead! Peter said, "God sent Jesus for all of us, to save us."

Many people in the crowd wanted to know what they were supposed to do. Peter said, "Change your ways and follow God. Be baptized! Ask God for forgiveness! Then you'll be filled with the Holy Spirit too!"

Three thousand people were baptized that day, and they were all filled with the Holy Spirit.

Hear: What language do you speak? Many people in the world speak more than one language. Ask someone you know to teach you some words in a language different from yours.

See: Look at a map of the world. Christians, people who believe in Jesus, live all over the world. Point to a country on the map. Look up pictures of Christians in their church in one of these countries. What looks familiar? What looks different?

Act: Find out the ways your church is involved in your community. What is one way you and your family can learn about other Christians both near and far away?

Living Together

Based on Acts 2:42–47; 4:32–35

When children move in next door, it takes time to get to know each other. As you play together, you learn how to get along. For example, you find ways to agree on the rules for a game you are playing. After all the people were baptized on Pentecost, they needed to learn how to get along.

The people who believed in Jesus wanted to be together. After they were baptized, they were filled with the Holy Spirit. But how were they going to live together day after day?

The disciples taught them about Jesus and what he taught. The people ate meals together like a family. They spent time together like a family. They also prayed for one another.

When one person was shivering in the cold, someone gave him a coat, and he was warm again. Perhaps another person was hungry. Someone gave her food, and they ate

together. When anything was needed, those who owned things sold them. They gave the money to the believers so that everyone had enough. No one was left out.

Because they were all faithful Jews, the people went to the temple every day. When they got home again, they ate together. They prayed, and ate, and laughed together. Everyone was happy and loved.

Other people watched them. More and more, people believed in Jesus. More and more, people were baptized. More and more, people showed everyone God's love by the way they lived.

Hear: What does it sound like when people are praising God? How do you praise God? Ask someone you love how it sounds when they praise God.

See: Who is in your church? Look around next time you are there. Draw a picture of the people you see. These people are part of your church family.

Act: Look at the pictures on these pages. How are the people showing love or helping others? What are some ways you can share with others?

Left Out

Based on Acts 6:1–7

If you have ever been the last one chosen for a team on the playground, you know how it feels to be left out. It helps when someone else stands up for you. Listen for some people who are left out and for who stands up for them in this story.

Some of the new believers who joined the disciples on Pentecost came from Greece. They spoke only Greek. Some were from Galilee and Palestine. They spoke only Aramaic. Now they were living together. They wanted to get along, but they didn't speak the same language.

As the days went by, a problem turned up. The people who gave out the food were leaving out the widows who spoke Greek. You remember that it was important that each person had enough food. This upset the people who spoke Greek.

When the twelve disciples heard about this, they told everyone, whether they spoke Greek or Aramaic, to come to a meeting.

"We're so busy," the disciples said. "We need to pray and tell people about Jesus. We don't have time to make sure everyone is getting enough food. Here's an idea: Choose seven people. Choose people you all like. Choose people who are smart and who love God. They will be in charge of giving out the food."

What a good idea! Everyone thought about who the seven people should be. Each one was liked by everyone. Each one was smart and loved God. And each one spoke Greek. These people were going to make sure that everyone had enough food and that no one was left out.

The disciples prayed for the seven people they had chosen. They put their hands on the shoulders of the seven people and blessed them. The disciples wanted these new leaders to know they had important work to do.

More and more, people believed in Jesus, too. Even some Jewish priests believed in Jesus.

Hear: When was the last time you heard someone complain? What did they complain about? Did you listen to them?

See: Who is left out? When you are with your friends, look around to see if anyone is left out.

Act: Reach out to a friend who is feeling left out. Ask what you can do to make your friend feel better.

Philip Baptizes a Traveler

Based on Acts 8:26–40

What do you do when you meet someone who is different from you? Philip once met a person who was different from him. He decided to get to know him better and tell him some good news.

After Pentecost, many believers went to other countries. Philip went to Samaria and told the people there about God. He also healed people. Many in Samaria became believers.

As Philip traveled from place to place, an angel said, "Go to the road that goes from Jerusalem to Gaza."

An Ethiopian man was also traveling on that road. He was in charge of all the money for the Ethiopian queen. He was returning from Jerusalem, where he had been to worship. As he rode in his carriage, he was reading the scroll of the prophet Isaiah.

The Holy Spirit said to Philip, "Catch up with that carriage."

When Philip reached the carriage, he asked, "Do you know what you're reading?"

"It's hard to understand without help," the Ethiopian man answered. "Can you help me?"

Philip got into the carriage. They read the scroll of Isaiah together. They read about the One God will send. They read how this man would be treated badly and killed.

The Ethiopian man asked, "Is Isaiah talking about himself or someone else?"

Philip told him about Jesus, how he lived and how he died. The Ethiopian learned the good news of how Jesus wanted people to live with others. Philip also wanted him to know how Jesus came back to life. The Ethiopian man was excited about this good news. As they were talking, the carriage passed by some water.

"Can I be baptized?" the Ethiopian man asked Philip.

The Ethiopian ordered the carriage to stop. The two men got out and walked to the water. Philip baptized the Ethiopian man. As soon as they stepped out of the water, God's Spirit took Philip to another place, where he preached about Jesus. The Ethiopian man went home and never saw Philip again.

Hear: When have you heard good news from someone you didn't know?

See: Imagine what the Ethiopian man told the queen of Ethiopia when he returned. Try drawing the different scenes in this story. Or tear up pieces of colored paper and make a collage.

Act: Find someone you don't know well. What good news can you tell your new friend?

Saul's Change of Heart

Based on Acts 9:1–19

When someone says something unexpected, we are surprised. Sometimes we are surprised by the way people act. Listen for surprises about Saul and Ananias.

Saul hated the believers in Jesus. He asked the high priest for a letter so that he could hunt down these believers and bring them back to Jerusalem to be arrested. He knew many had gone to Damascus. That is where Saul and the men with him were going. But God had a surprise for Saul on the road to Damascus.

When the travelers were coming close to Damascus, a bright light from the sky circled Saul. It was so bright that Saul fell down.

"Saul, why are you so mean to me?" asked a voice from above.

"Who are you?" Saul asked.

"I'm Jesus. When you are mean to the people who believe in me, you are being mean to me, too. Go to Damascus. I'll tell you what to do when you get there."

The men with Saul saw the bright light and heard the voice. They helped Saul stand up. When Saul opened his eyes, he couldn't see. The people with Saul had to lead him to Damascus.

At the same time, Jesus talked to a man named Ananias, who believed in Jesus and lived in Damascus.

"Saul is in town. I told him that a man named Ananias would help him."

This scared Ananias.

"I know about Saul," he said. "He wants to arrest me and anyone who believes in Jesus. He is dangerous."

But Jesus said, "It will be fine. I have chosen Saul to do important work for me. He will not be mean to you."

Ananias went to the house on Straight Street where Saul was staying. He touched Saul's eyes and said, "Brother Saul, Jesus sent me to make you see again. You are now filled with the Holy Spirit."

Flakes like fish scales fell from Saul's eyes. He could see! Then Ananias baptized Saul. From that day on Saul stopped being mean to people who believed in Jesus.

Instead, he told everyone about the good news of Jesus. Saul, whose heart had been changed by Jesus, was better known after that as Paul.

Hear: Pretend you are Ananias and you are telling your friends about helping Saul. What will you say? What do you think they will say?

See: In the story, Saul couldn't see. Walk around your home with your eyes closed. Be careful! What is it like when you can't see?

Act: Saul stopped being mean to the people who believed in Jesus after Jesus spoke to him. How does knowing about Jesus help you be kinder and more helpful to others?

Tabitha Rejoins Her Friends

Based on Acts 9:36–43

When you miss someone you love, you may be very sad. This is how Jesus' friends felt before Jesus came back to life.

Tabitha loved Jesus very much. She did all she could for people who needed help. She was also very good at sewing clothes. She made clothes for widows who needed new clothes but had no money. She worked hard to make sure that everyone knew about Jesus' love. Everyone loved Tabitha.

Then Tabitha got very sick and died.

Everyone was so sad. They couldn't believe that Tabitha was gone. Peter, one of Jesus' friends, was in a nearby town. He was telling people about Jesus. When Tabitha's friends heard that Peter was near, they went to get him.

"Come with us right away," they told Peter. "Tabitha died, and we are all sad. Please come pray for her."

Peter went with them. When they got to the house, Peter saw how sad Tabitha's

friends were. They told him all how much they loved Tabitha. They showed Peter the clothing that Tabitha had made for others.

Peter said, "Let me see Tabitha."

They took him to the room where her body was. Peter told them to wait outside. He knelt by the bed and prayed. When he stood up, Peter said, "Tabitha, get up."

Tabitha opened her eyes!

"Let me help you stand," Peter said as he took Tabitha's hand.

They went to Tabitha's friends. Her friends were so excited when they saw her alive!

People heard about Tabitha and Peter, and even more people believed in Jesus.

Hear: What would you do if you heard someone crying?

See: Make the faces that you think Tabitha's friends made. How did they look at the beginning of the story? How did they look at the end of the story?

Act: Is there someone you miss? Write a letter to that person to say you miss her or him. Tell that person how happy you will be when you see him or her again.

Lydia Meets Paul

Based on Acts 16:11–15

Sometimes we find good things in unexpected places. When we listen to God, we should be ready to be surprised like that. What good thing happens in this story?

Paul and his friends traveled from city to city to tell people the good news about Jesus. One of the first cities they went to was Philippi, a city ruled by the Romans. Paul found that not many Jews lived in Philippi, so there was no synagogue.

Where do people go to worship God? he wondered.

Worshipers of God gathered to pray on a riverbank outside the city. Some women were praying there when Paul and his friends arrived. Paul sat down to talk with the women.

One woman was named Lydia. She sold purple cloth to kings, queens, and other rich people. This made her very wealthy. Lydia was curious about what Paul told them. She wanted to know more about Jesus. She heard the good news, and she was excited!

"Paul," she asked, "would you baptize me and everyone who lives in my house?"

Paul did baptize them all. Then Lydia said, "You don't know many people here. Now you know that I am a believer in Jesus. Please stay at my house."

Paul and his friends stayed with Lydia as long as they were in Philippi. They were able to tell many more people about Jesus and how he wanted them to treat other people.

Hear: Where do you hear people talk about Jesus? What do you think it would be like to tell someone who had never heard of Jesus about him?

See: Close your eyes and imagine that you are sitting on the bank of a river. If you were praying with Lydia, what would you pray to God?

Act: Where do you like to pray in your home? Why is that a good place to talk with God? Go there now and pray.

Paul and Silas in Prison

Based on Acts 16:16–40

Sometimes you get in trouble even if you do the right thing.

Paul and Silas were still in Philippi at Lydia's house. Each day, they walked through the marketplace on the way to the riverbank to pray. They saw a woman telling fortunes. She was a slave, so people paid her owners instead of paying her.

When the woman saw Paul and Silas, she shouted, "Those men are servants of the true God!"

Finally, Paul had enough of her yelling and said, "In the name of Jesus Christ, stop!"

The woman did, but now she couldn't tell fortunes either.

Her owners were angry that she couldn't earn money for them. They dragged Paul and Silas to court. "These men are making trouble. They are telling people to do things that are against Roman ways." Paul and Silas weren't making trouble. But the judges listened to the slave owners. They threw Paul and Silas in jail.

Paul and Silas sang hymns and prayed to God until early in the morning. God heard them and sent an earthquake. It shook the building so hard that the prisoners' chains fell off. But not one prisoner left!

The shaking and noise woke the prison guard. When he saw the open doors, he thought everyone had escaped. He was afraid that he would lose his job.

But Paul yelled, "Don't worry! We're all here!"

The prison guard ran to Paul and Silas. "How can I know about your God?"

Paul and Silas told the prison guard about Jesus and the amazing things he did. They went home with the prison guard. They baptized him and everyone who lived in his house. Then they ate together.

The next day, the judges told Paul and Silas that they were free. They said that they were sorry for putting them in prison.

Paul and Silas went to Lydia's house to say good-bye. Then they were on their way.

Hear: Paul and Silas sang hymns. What songs about God or Jesus do you know?

See: What do you think the woman looked like before and after Paul helped her?

Act: Paul and Silas surprised the prison guard by staying in the prison. Today, do something nice for someone who isn't expecting it!

A Letter from a Friend

Based on 2 Timothy 1:1–7

Have you ever gotten a letter or a card in the mail? Not many people write letters today. But in Bible times, letters written on scrolls were important. Getting a letter was exciting.

Paul's good friend Timothy was a leader of the church in Ephesus. Like many places, the church people in Ephesus were often treated badly by others. Paul knew that Timothy was sad and needed to remember their friendship. Because Paul was in prison and couldn't go to Ephesus, he wrote letters to Timothy. Two of them are in the Bible. This is the beginning of the Second Letter to Timothy.

"From Paul.

"To my dear friend Timothy.

"The peace of God and Jesus to you. I miss you, and I think about you a lot. I pray for you all the time. I heard that you're sad right now because it is hard to speak for Jesus. I wish I could see you and know that you are all right.

"I think a lot about your strong faith. It reminds me of your grandmother Lois and your mother, Eunice. I am sure that they passed their love for Jesus on to you. Thinking about you makes me happy. I hope my letter makes you feel better. God loves you. God is with you no matter what. Please don't forget that.

"Even in prison I know that God is with me. You received God's Spirit when we placed our hands on your head and prayed for you. God's Spirit is not quiet, but loving and powerful. You have that Spirit now."

Hear: Have someone you love read this letter out loud to you. Ask them to replace Timothy's name with yours. Ask them to put the names of people you love in place of "Lois" and "Eunice." How did you feel as you listened to this letter?

See: When you go to church next time, look around for people who you think have God's Spirit, people who are kind or people who are doing things for others.

Act: Write a letter, or get help writing a letter, to someone. Remind this person of your love. Let this person know God's love is for everyone.

One Church

Based on 1 Corinthians 12:12–31

Today, people get text messages from friends. People used to write letters. Many years ago, a church community received a letter from the apostle Paul.

After Pentecost, the church began to spread beyond Jerusalem. Some followers of Jesus started a church in the city of Corinth. This church was like one big family, but sometimes they quarreled. One day, they began to argue about who was the best follower of Jesus. The argument went on and on. Some people sent a message to their friend Paul asking for help.

Paul couldn't come to them so he wrote a letter. When the letter arrived, the people gathered together to hear what Paul had to say.

"Dear Friends,

"Our church is like a body. A body is made up of different parts: head, legs, arms, feet. Each part has a different job to do.

"Imagine if the whole body were a giant mouth, how would it see? If the body were just an eyeball, how would it move around?

"The ear cannot say to the mouth, 'I don't need you.' The head won't say to the nose, 'Go away, I don't want you.' How silly that would be.

"Each person in the church is like a part of the body. Each one of us is important. We each have a job to do. But we can work together. We can help one another. Remember, dear friends, we need one another because we are each part of God's church.

"Your friend, Paul"

The people thought about Paul's words.

The people realized it was silly to argue about who was the best follower of

Jesus. They were each important! They each had a job to do, and they needed one another.

They knew that if they worked together they would be able to do wonderful things for God. And that's what they did!

Hear: What did you learn about living as the church from this story?

See: What pictures did you imagine in your head as you read Paul's letter?

Act: What special gifts and talents do you have? How can you use these gifts in the church?

God's Gift of Love

Based on 1 Corinthians 13:1–13

When the church was just beginning, a man named Paul traveled to many different places to start new churches. He told people about Jesus. He would stay in each city for a while and then move on.

Sometimes the people in these churches didn't get along. Everyone had different ideas about how to follow Jesus. Sometimes they quarreled and argued.

Paul heard that the people in the city of Corinth were arguing with one another. He wanted to teach them how to live together in peace. He was far away from Corinth, so he sent a letter to remind them about God's love.

"Dear Friends in Corinth,

"Let me tell you again about God's gift of love.

"I may speak with a voice as beautiful as an angel's. But if I do not have love, I sound like a clanging gong to God.

"I may be able to answer the hardest questions. But if I do not have love, all my knowledge means nothing to God.

"I may even give my whole life to God. But if I do not have love, then nothing I do matters to God.

"Love is patient and kind. Love does not boast or brag. Love is not rude and doesn't always want its own way. Love doesn't stay angry for a long time.

"Love grows in the truth.

"Many things come and go, but God's love never ends.

"God gives us three gifts. They are faith, hope, and love. The greatest of these is love.

"Let us show this kind of love to others every day.

"Your friend, Paul"

The people in Corinth saved this letter and shared it with others. After many years, it became part of our Bible. We can also learn from it about living as the church.

Hear: How does Paul want the Corinthians to live?

See: What does love look like to you?

Act: How did Jesus show the kind of love Paul wrote about? What is one way you could show love this week?

You Are Part of the Body of Christ

Based on Ephesians 4:1–16

Before phones and computers, people communicated over long distances by letter. Many letters were saved and are in the Bible. Some letters were written to persons. Other letters were written to a church. This letter was written in the name of the apostle Paul to the church in Ephesus. You can read more about Paul in other stories in this book. This is how the letter begins:

"To the people who follow Jesus in Ephesus.

"Grace and peace to you from God and Jesus.

"You have been called by God to be a follower of Jesus. Live so you show that God is in you. Treat others with kindness. Think of what you can do for others before you think about yourself. Love one another.

"Be together in peace. The church is one body, and God has given you one hope. There is one God and one baptism. Jesus Christ has given each of you gifts to help you spread God's love. Some have the gift to speak God's word to you. Some have the gift to tell people about God and Jesus Christ. Others have the gift to teach. Christ gives a gift to each one. God uses everyone's gifts. With your gifts you can work together to help one another do God's work in the world.

"When you speak the truth to others in loving ways, you will all grow in Christ. So each of you should do your part as you are joined together in the body of Christ. You are the hands and feet, and Christ is the head of the body of Christ. Everyone is important, and no one is too small to help the body of Christ."

Hear: What are some of your talents and gifts?

See: How do you use your talents and gifts to help others and to show God's love in the world?

Act: Talk with your family about ways you can work together to show God's love in the world.

You Can Do It!

Based on Hebrews 12:1–2

Have you ever thought you couldn't do something because it was going to be hard? It can be hard to take a test in school. It can be hard to get along with a friend. It can be hard to run for a long time. Sometimes just being you can be hard.

Letters in the Bible are usually written to a person or a church. But the letter to the Hebrews was written to all who believed in Jesus Christ. It seems that many of them were having a hard time. People who didn't believe in Jesus were mean to them. The Roman rulers hunted them down. This letter has words to encourage them and help them to be brave. Perhaps they will help you to be brave and do hard things too.

"Let's all run the race of life God has given us. We can do this because a great cloud of witnesses have done it before us.

"Who is in that cloud of witnesses? God told Moses to free God's people, the Israelites who were slaves in Egypt. Moses was afraid of the Egyptian pharaoh. But God gave him courage to lead the people to the Promised Land.

"Then remember Ruth. She stayed with her mother-in-law, Naomi. They went back to Bethlehem, a new home for Ruth. It was not easy for her to go to a strange land.

"Remember Miriam, David, Samuel, Esther, and all the prophets of God; they are all in the cloud of witnesses. Each one of them gives us courage to be strong people of God and followers of Jesus today."

The letter to the Hebrews says to keep trying, even when it is hard. Even when we think we can't, we must try. Above all, we keep our eyes on Jesus. Jesus loves us. Jesus believes in us. With Jesus we can do anything, even if it is hard!

Hear: Think of a time when you had to do something hard. Who asked you to do this? Why was it hard?

See: Who are some people in your life who help you do something hard? They are in your great cloud of witnesses. How do they help you?

Act: How will you keep your eyes on Jesus so that he can help you do something hard?

A Loving Heart Helps Others

Based on James 1:19–27; 2:1–7

Parents and teachers tell you many important things. I bet your list is really long! How do you remember them all? Here's a letter from a man named James, who wrote it when the church was just getting started. He wanted the people in the church to remember what Jesus had taught about how to treat other people. Here's what he said:

"Brothers and Sisters,

"It's not always easy living together in a family at home or at church. So if something happens that makes you angry, pause for a minute and listen before you talk. It's good to slow down, to stop and think. When we listen to others, we learn about them. We learn why they do or say certain things.

"Another thing to remember about hearing and doing is this: Look at yourself in the mirror. What do you see? Do you see someone who knows the right thing to do in his head but forgets and does the wrong thing? Or do you see someone who knows the right thing to do and does it? God wants the things you know and the things you do to go together.

"The third thing to remember is about how you treat other people. Think about this and what you would do. Let's say you get to church, and you see two people in the room. One is dressed in really nice clothes and smells like lavender. Then you see someone whose clothes aren't as nice, whose shoes have holes in the soles. And worst of all, this person needs a good warm bath. Remember, God wants us to treat all people the same way. God wants us to welcome everyone and help them all the same.

"And finally, remember to love all people. You will meet many different people. People of all different colors. People of different shapes and sizes. People of different religions. People who should not be hurt because of who they love. These people may need your help. Be kind. Say nice things to others. Accept them for who they are. Being a friend is the easiest way to help others.

"God wants us to treat all people with love. And I know you will."

Hear: Try listening to those around you. Hear their stories about life.

See: What do you see happening around you that hurts others? What do you see happening around you that helps others?

Act: Who are some people you know who need your listening ear and your acts of kindness and love?

Light and Darkness

Based on 1 John 1:5–10

The next three stories all come from books written by a person named John. They are letters with a lot of advice, things the writer wants you to remember. Imagine if your grandparent or aunt or uncle or teacher wrote you a letter or sent you a text message about something really important about how you were supposed to live.

Here's what John said:

"It's been a long time since Jesus lived among us. So I wanted to write to you and help you remember some of the things he taught us. Before I tell you these things, imagine yourself on top of a hill on a warm summer day. Flowers and tall grass are all around you blowing in the breeze. The sun is shining and feels so nice and warm. You shut your eyes and lift your face toward the sun. It feels so good that you never want to leave that place. Now imagine that you are in a very dark room. It doesn't feel like before. Someone who loves you very much brings in a candle. The light from that candle brightens the room, and the room is not as dark as before.

"Jesus taught us that God wants us to live in the light, not the dark. To live in the light means to live in love. God is light because God is love. Jesus taught us to love God and to love others. Jesus also wants us to remember that we are not perfect. We make mistakes. When we tell God about our mistakes and ask for forgiveness, God will always forgive us. When we pray to God and love one another, we are living in the light.

"Light will always be stronger than darkness. Even the smallest candle can brighten a dark room. You can make this world brighter by loving God and loving one another."

Hear: Think of a time when you made a mistake. Did you say you were sorry? Did you tell God you were sorry?

See: How can you live in the light with God and with others?

Act: Make a prayer journal with a pad of paper. Decorate it with markers and stickers. Write your prayers to God in it. Tell God about how you are going to live in the light.

Things We Do and Things We Say

Based on 1 John 3:18–24

Have you ever told someone, "You are my friend" and then you did something that wasn't very friendly? That's something John wrote about in one of his letters. Imagine he was writing his letter to you!

"Dear Children,

"I have been thinking a lot about what it means to say, 'I love you.' Three little words that mean so much. Have you ever heard someone say, 'Actions speak louder than words'? What do you think it means when someone says that?

"Sometimes we say one thing and then do something different. Have you ever made a promise and then not been able to keep it? Remember that what you do is as important as what you say. So if you say that you love someone or you tell someone he is your friend, then you show it. You are kind to others. When you see a child on the playground who needs a friend, you offer to play with her.

"You can show that God is love when you treat others with love and kindness. God knows that we all make mistakes. God asks us to keep trying."

Hear: Have you heard someone say one thing and then do something different?

See: Who are some people you know that need to be shown love?

Act: What can you do to show your family and friends that you love them?

Making Smart Choices

Based on 3 John 11

Sometimes it's hard to make good decisions. Someone may want you to do something that might not be smart or right. Knowing what to do that is right is something everyone knows about, even your parents. Here's what John had to say about it in one of his letters. It's really amazing that something written so long ago is still important today.

"Dear Friend,

"I know that I have been reminding you about a lot of things in the letters I have been writing. There's one thing more I want you to remember. It's really a small thing, but it is very important. When you see someone doing something that you know is not smart or good, don't do it. Say someone wants you to cheat on a test. You know that's not a good thing. You can say no! If someone wants you to join in and treat another child badly, you can say no!

"God is very happy when we do things that are good. Doing good things helps the world become a better place. God asks that we care for one another and do good things to help others. Helping set the table for dinner is a good thing to do. Making sure your pet always has clean water is a good thing to do. Making wise choices is a good thing. Doing good things helps us to see God.

"The world is full of people. Some of them are very good. Some are not always good. Stay with those who do good things."

Hear: Who are your friends? What are some of the good things you do together?

See: Who can you talk to when someone asks you to do something bad?

Act: What can you do to make the world a better place?

Listening to Jesus

Reading the stories about Jesus in the New Testament is not a small job; it's a big job. There are many different stories. When you read them, you begin to wonder if there is one really important story. Is there one thing that I'm supposed to remember? What is the most important thing Jesus wants me to remember to do as I live my life?

In this section are some stories that might be a top-ten list of things Jesus wants us to remember. So count them down:

#10 Remember these two things: Love God and love your neighbor.

#9 Children are a special blessing in this world.

#8 Don't worry about anything.

#7 Remember to pray.

#6 Jesus is the bread of life.

#5 Jesus is the light of the world and wants us to be his light and his salt.

#4 Jesus is like a vine, and we are the branches.

#3 Remember, Jesus said that he is the good shepherd.

#2 Take care of others.

#1 Remember to bless and be blessed.

A Blessing Map

Based on Matthew 5:1–12

When you go on a trip, you look at a map to find the best road to follow. Here's a story about how Jesus gave his disciples a map for how they were to live. Jesus had been teaching and healing people. He invited twelve people to be his disciples.

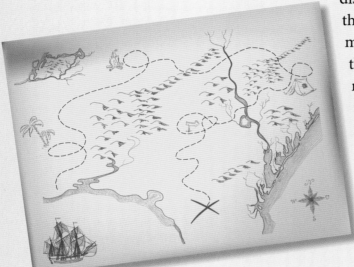

He told them important things to remember, a kind of map for disciples. They are called the *Beatitudes*, a word that means "blessings." Here they are written as if Jesus were talking to you, as one of his disciples.

"You are blessed when you take time to talk with God, to say thank you, or help me, or please remember, or I am sorry.

"You are following me when you see something wrong or someone being treated badly and you do something to help.

"When you see a person or an animal who is lost or homeless or without friends, and you and your family help out, you are blessed.

"When you are hungry for everyone to have enough food to eat, then you are on the right road. When you are thirsty and know that some children need clean water to drink, and you save your money to help, you are blessed.

"When you see a classmate sitting alone and you join her, you are following me.

"When your heart is open to love others, then you will know what God looks like.

"When you are a peacemaker, helping people learn how to listen to one another and not fight, you are living like you are God's child.

"When you see things that aren't good and you work to make them better, you are on the right road.

"When you try and do these things, you will be blessed and happy."

Hear: What other things do you think Jesus told his disciples that we need to remember today?

See: Draw a picture or make a collage that tells a story about a time when you followed Jesus.

Act: Which of the things Jesus said have you tried? What happened?

Seeing Jesus

Based on Matthew 25:31–46

When you leave to go to school, your parent might say something important to remember. "Have a good day; give a good day." "Ask a good question."

After Jesus entered Jerusalem for the last time and before he ate the Passover meal with his disciples, he taught things he wanted people to remember about how to live. If he were telling you this story today, it might sound like this.

"I want you to remember four things.

"The **first** is I love you.

"The **second** is *Love me* with all your heart.

"A parent or family member says 'I love you.' They show their love this way. When you are hungry, there is food to eat. When you come in from playing outside, there is water to drink. When you get ready for school, there are clean clothes ready to wear. If you are ever in trouble and need someone to talk to, they are there and ready to listen.

"The **third** important thing is that you can't really see me, but you *can see me* in others when you do kind things for them:

"When you help serve a meal at a homeless shelter, spend time with a friend who is sad, save money to give to a group that helps people, sit with someone at school who is eating alone, help your parent buy clothes or toys for children in a homeless shelter or refugee center, make friends with a child with autism, or help someone in a wheelchair, I am there.

"The *circle of your love* can be very big.

"And the **fourth** thing to remember is *I am there* watching your circle of love grow!"

Hear: What new ideas for living like Jesus do you hear in this story?

See: Try drawing your circle of love. Who is in it? Who is not? Who can you add?

Act: Living Waters for the World (http://livingwatersfortheworld.org) makes sure that all God's children have clean water. Have a quarter jar at home and church. Every time you eat a meal away from home, put in a quarter. When the jar is full, send the money to Living Waters for the World or another service group.

We see Jesus when . . .

The Good Shepherd

Based on John 10:11–16

"I'm short." "I'm a good soccer player." "I like music." People learn about us by the things we say! Everyone seemed to know Jesus' name. But he also wanted them to know more than that. Jesus wanted people he met to know something about him. So he used things he saw around him to describe himself. This is the first of four stories. In this one he told people he was a good shepherd.

Jesus knew many shepherds. They were all over the hillsides. Shepherds made their living by caring for their sheep. They guided their flocks to water and to grass and to safe places for the night. Jesus spent time with them and saw how they cared about their sheep. People knew about good shepherds and how they cared for their sheep. So Jesus talked about himself as a good shepherd.

"I am the good shepherd. I care deeply for all the sheep in my flock. I know what they need to be healthy and happy. I know my sheep, and my sheep know me. In the same way, God knows the shepherd, and I know God.

"I have other sheep, who do not belong to this flock. I care for them and give them what they need too. I call to them, and they listen to my voice. One day, there will be only one flock with one good shepherd."

Jesus also warned the listeners about bad shepherds. "Beware of those who will pretend to be the good shepherd. They will do some of the same things that I do. However, they do only what helps them, not what helps the sheep. They do not own the sheep. When they see a wolf, they run away to save themselves. Then the wolf will steal the weak sheep, and the flock will not be whole. The bad shepherd pretends to care about the sheep. In the end, the bad shepherd will lead you to bad places.

"Follow me, listen to my voice, and I will care for you."

Hear: How does it feel to know that Jesus is your shepherd and guide?

See: What things or people can distract you or pull you away from following Jesus?

Act: Do you feel Jesus guiding you in your life? How can you respond?

The True Vine

Based on John 15:1–8

Have you ever seen a field filled with grapevines? As Jesus and the disciples walked from village to village, they saw many fields of grapes called vineyards. He used the image of grapevines to teach about himself.

Jesus said, "I am the true vine, and God is the owner of the vineyard. All the branches that grow from me will live and bear grapes. God removes the dead branches to keep the healthy branches connected to me.

"You have been shaped by the good news that I taught you. Stay connected to me in the same way that I live in you. Branches do not live and produce fruit unless they are connected to the vine. You can do nothing if you are not alive in me.

"I am the vine, and you are the branches. Like the branches on the vine, as long as you are connected to me you will live and do loving things. If you stay connected to me, ask for what you need and you will receive it. You love God when you are connected to me. You remember God when your life bears fruit and you are my followers."

Hear: What do you think Jesus means when he says we are connected to him like branches to the vine?

See: What kinds of loving things have you seen today? What have you done today that is loving?

Act: What do you do to stay connected to Jesus?

The Light of the World

Based on John 8:12

If someone asked you, "Who are you?" How would you answer? "I am . . ." Would you tell them your name or something about yourself? Jesus wanted to tell his friends about himself. There was more to him than his friends could see. So he tried to use something familiar—light to help people know more about him.

Jesus was teaching and healing in Galilee and Jerusalem. He did some amazing things, like healing a man who couldn't walk. He fed a whole crowd with a child's lunch. He walked on water to meet the disciples who were in a boat during a storm on a lake. Some might have said that Jesus was someone who fed people. Others would remember that Jesus was a healer. And the disciples knew that he was someone who could do things no one else could do.

Jesus might have said to them, "Yes, I am a healer. Yes, I am the one who can make five loaves and two fish feed a whole crowd. Yes, I am the one who walked out to the disciples on the water. But I am more than each of these things."

Jesus wanted people to think about what they had seen and heard about him. When he was teaching in the temple, he told them, "I am the light of the world." He wanted them to remember what he was teaching about loving God and loving others. "If you follow me and remember what I have been teaching, then you also will be lights in the world."

Jesus knew that the dark can be scary. When it's dark, we can't see a path to follow. In the dark, it's hard to see if someone is close by. But with light, life is good. Jesus is the light of the world.

Hear: Why do you think Jesus talked about light and darkness?

See: How does it feel to know that Jesus, the light of the world, is with you?

Act: What are some ways you can be a light in the world?

The Bread of Life

Based on John 6:35–37

There is something that people all over the world eat. Think about it! Sometimes it is long and skinny, or round, or even a rectangle. It has different names, like naan, chapatti, pita, tortillas, and bagels. But it's all the same. Yes, it's bread. Here's the fourth story Jesus told about himself. Here he used something really familiar—bread—to help people know more about him.

Jesus shared a lot of meals during his life. He ate meals at home with his family. He ate meals on the road with his friends. He ate fish on the beach after his friends brought in the day's catch. He ate meals at parties and weddings. He even made sure that they had wine to keep the party going! And there are more stories about Jesus feeding people, stories you have read in this book. Which ones do you remember?

After feeding a very large crowd with only five loaves of bread and two fish, Jesus was talking with his disciples. They were trying to figure out how God wanted them to live. They asked Jesus, "What does God want from us? And what kinds of things are you doing that will help us know how we are to live?" They remembered stories they passed down from their parents and grandparents. "We know that many years ago, after they left Egypt, people were hungry in the wilderness. We have been told that God fed them with manna, bread that came from heaven."

Jesus said, "You are right. God fed them bread. God gave them life."

And then it was like a light went off for the disciples. They told Jesus, "We want bread like that."

Jesus looked at them and smiled. He said, "I am the bread of life. I am the nourishment that feeds you. I am the force that gives you life. Anyone who follows me will not be hungry. If you listen to what I am saying and do what I have been teaching, you will not be thirsty. Everyone whom God sends will come to me, and

I will turn no one away." Jesus let his friends think about what he said for a few minutes, and then they started walking again.

Hear: Why do you think we have so many stories about Jesus eating with people?

See: Think about meals you have with family and friends. How do they give you life?

Act: How do you feed your spirit with the Bread of Life?

Salt and Light for Our World

Based on Matthew 5:13–16

Just a little salt can make many foods taste better. Eat some plain popcorn. Then shake a little salt on it and taste it again. Taste the difference? In a dark room, only one candle can spread a lot of light. Jesus talked about salt and light to his disciples.

Jesus had much to teach the disciples so that they could help with his work. Perhaps one day one of them said, "But Jesus, I don't understand what you want us to do in the world."

Jesus answered, "When you are my followers, you make a difference in the world. Be like salt for the earth. Salt gives foods flavor and brings out the goodness in them. It also preserves food so that you can keep it longer. But if salt is no longer salty, what good is it? It is no longer useful and will be thrown out.

"Be like light for the world. A bright light on the top of a mountain cannot be hidden. People don't light candles and cover them up. Instead, they set the candle on a table where it can light the way for everyone. In the same way, let the light of God's love shine on the people around you. Let them see your good actions and praise God in heaven."

Hear: Why does Jesus tell his followers to be like salt and light for the world?

See: Where do you see people being like salt and light around you?

Act: How might you shine the light of God for others?

The Lord's Prayer

Based on Luke 11:1–4

When do you pray to God? What do you say? Jesus' disciples wanted to know how to pray.

Jesus often went off by himself to pray to God. One day, when he returned from praying, one of the disciples said, "John the baptizer taught his disciples to pray. Why don't you teach us to pray as you do?"

Jesus said to them, "When you pray, pray like this:

"Our God your name is forever holy.

"May your plan for your world—to be a place of healing and freedom for everyone—be our work on earth just as it is in heaven.

"Give us what we need for today.

"When we do something that is wrong, forgive us. And help us remember to do that for others.

"Don't ever let us do something that is wrong. Amen."

Hear: When do you hear people pray a prayer almost like this?

See: What does it mean to you to pray these words?

Act: What other prayers do you say?

Jesus Blesses the Children

Based on Mark 10:13–16

In Jesus' time, people thought children weren't important. But Jesus thought that they were very important. One day, Jesus and his disciples walked from one town to another. Crowds of people came to see them. The crowds made it difficult for everyone to get close to Jesus.

Some parents brought their children to Jesus so that he could bless them. The disciples were annoyed that the parents and children were coming to Jesus.

"Jesus is far too busy to bother with a bunch of children," they complained to one another. "He has more important things to do."

They tried to stop the children and their parents. "Go away!" they cried. "Look at all these people! Jesus is much too busy to see you today."

The children were disappointed. They wanted to see Jesus.

The parents felt sad. They wanted Jesus to bless their children. Jesus was upset when he saw his friends pushing the children and their parents away.

"Let the little children come to me," he said. "I want to be with them. Don't keep them from me!"

The children ran up to Jesus and gathered around him laughing.

The disciples were puzzled. "Why is Jesus spending time with children? Look at all these people. They are more important."

Jesus could see that his friends didn't understand.

"You think that children are not important," said Jesus. "You are wrong. Children are important to God. They can teach us about loving and trusting and living in God's ways. Watch and learn from them."

Then Jesus hugged each child, placed his hands on each head, and blessed each one.

Hear: What do you think the children thought when Jesus told the disciples to let them get close?

See: What do you think the disciples did the next time parents brought children to Jesus?

Act: Do you know any children with special needs? What do you think Jesus would say to them? What can you do to help these children feel loved and included?

Don't Worry

Based on Matthew 6:25–34

Jesus had a group of special friends who followed him from place to place. They wanted to learn how to follow in God's way. Let's listen in as Jesus teaches them.

One day, Jesus and his disciples sat down on the side of a hill. Jesus wanted to teach them about God and living in God's loving ways.

"Don't worry about anything," Jesus told them. "You don't have to worry about food to eat. Don't worry about your clothes. There is far more to life than food and clothes. God loves you and knows what you need."

At that moment, some birds flew over their heads. They swooped and soared in the sky. Beautiful birdsong filled the air. Jesus smiled and pointed to them.

"Look at those birds," he said. "They don't plant food, harvest the grain, or store it in barns. Still God gives those birds plenty to eat. They don't have to worry. If God looks after the birds, surely God will look after you. You are worth more than birds, so stop worrying. God loves you and knows what you need."

Jesus pointed to the wild flowers on the hillside. "Look at all those flowers. See how they grow. They don't spin cloth or sew clothes, but look how beautiful God makes them. They don't have to worry. Even the great King Solomon didn't have clothes as beautiful as these flowers. If God clothes the wild flowers, surely God will look after you, so stop worrying. God loves you and knows what you need.

"People who don't know God worry a lot about what food they will eat or what clothes they will wear. You don't have to be like them. You won't miss out. God loves you and knows what you need.

"Instead of fussing and worrying about these things, spend your time doing what God wants. Don't worry about what will happen tomorrow. Remember God loves you and knows what you need."

Hear: What did Jesus want his disciples to understand?

See: Think about the flowers in your neighborhood. Look at one and describe the clothes God gives it to wear.

Act: What do you worry about? What do you think Jesus would say to you? What can you do with your worries?

Remember to Love!

Based on Matthew 22:36–40

It's often hard to remember the right thing to do. Sometimes people write something they want to remember on a sticky note. Teachers used to pin notes on children with things for a parent to remember. Now they probably send an email or text. Here's a story about something Jesus wanted everyone to always remember.

Jesus had been teaching people about who he was and what they needed to know about how to live. A person who knew a lot about laws came to him and asked a question.

"Teacher, what is the most important commandment in all the laws we have been given? There are so many. But which one is the one we should always remember and never forget?"

Jesus was glad the legal expert had asked him this question. He paused for a minute. He knew which one was most important. It was very old, a scripture he had known since he was a small boy. It was from the book of Deuteronomy.

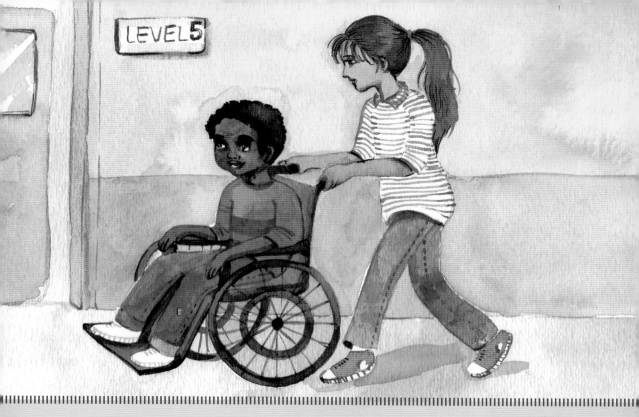

It was called the *Shema*, which means "to hear or listen." It was easy to remember, because he had been saying it twice a day all of his life. It was written on his heart and remembered in his head.

Jesus told him, "Love God with your heart and with your eyes and ears, your hands, every part of your body. This is the first commandment and the most important one."

Jesus knew that the legal expert would know this important commandment. Then Jesus surprised him and said, "There's a second one that is a lot like the first one. Remember to love other people, care for other people just like you take care of yourself."

Hear: Try saying the most important commandment once in the morning and once at night this week: I will love God with all my heart.

See: Use your eyes today. Where do you see people loving God? Where do you see people loving and helping other people?

Act: What are some ways that you can love God?

How Big Is God's Love?

You've come to the last story! Do you have a favorite? Is there anything that connects these stories?

Imagine a big, thick, warm quilt. And the colors? Fabrics in every color of the rainbow are in this quilt of God's love—magenta and brown, green and yellow, red and black, turquoise and purple. Every color is needed.

This quilt tells a story. Each square reminds you of God's love.

One square helps you remember how God created the waters and the land, plants and animals, and us.

Another square shows Miriam and Moses leading God's people out of slavery to freedom. God's love followed them with manna to eat and water to drink.

Find the square with Jonah. God had a hard time getting Jonah to understand about loving people who were different from him, people he didn't like.

When you don't feel brave, look at Queen Esther. She knew that God loved her, and this love made her strong enough to stand up to the king and save her people.

When you wonder what God wants you to do in this world, remember Micah. He reminded God's people that when we love God we treat people fairly.

John the baptizer saw God's love coming down when he baptized Jesus.

Jesus helped people know how much God wanted them to love everyone. That included people who were differently abled and others who were different from them. Jesus shared bread with people whom others didn't like.

When people were trying to understand what God's realm looked like, Jesus told them to talk with children, because the children already knew.

After Jesus returned to God, God's Spirit stayed with everyone. She reminded them how to share food and share what they had with others who needed it.

When we love God, we take care of God's world.

When we love God, we share God's love with others.

When we love God, we are kind and helpful.

God's love is very big. How big is your love?

Hear: What words from God would you like to hear God say?

See: What other stories would you like to add to the quilt?

Act: How can you show God's love?

Contributors

Kimber-lee D. Adams is Associate Pastor of First Presbyterian Church in Bloomington, Indiana.

Shawna Bowman is Pastor of Friendship Presbyterian Church in Chicago, Illinois.

Lora Burge works as Coordinator of the Presbyterian Peace Fellowship's Columbia Accompaniment Program and as Chaplain at Ann and Robert H. Lurie Children's Hospital of Chicago, Illinois.

Elizabeth F. Caldwell is an author, editor, and curriculum consultant and teaches as Adjunct Faculty at Vanderbilt Divinity School. She is Professor Emerita of McCormick Theological Seminary.

Megan Cochran is Associate Pastor of Lake View Presbyterian Church in Chicago, Illinois.

Shelley C. Donaldson is Senior High and Confirmation Youth Coordinator at Fourth Presbyterian Church in Chicago, Illinois.

Jeffrey Fox-Kline is Associate Pastor of Covenant Presbyterian Church in Madison, Wisconsin.

M. Evelyn Graham works in the Pastoral Care Department at Monroe Carell Jr. Children's Hospital at Vanderbilt in Nashville, Tennessee, and is in ordination process with the Presbyterian Church (U.S.A.).

Sharon Harding is a librarian at Athabasca University and a Christian educator and curriculum writer who has worked in ministries with children/youth at churches in Quebec and Alberta in Canada.

Theodore Hiebert is Francis A. McGaw Professor of Old Testament at McCormick Theological Seminary in Chicago, Illinois.

Cathy Caldwell Hoop is Pastor of Grace Presbyterian Church in Tuscaloosa, Alabama.

Jenny Hubbard is Director of Children and Family Ministries at Knox Presbyterian Church in Naperville, Illinois.

Jennifer J. Ikoma-Motzko was Senior Minister of the Japanese Baptist Church of Seattle until July 2014 and is now a stay-at-home mom.

Veronica M. Johnson is Senior Director of Admissions and Enrollment at McCormick Theological Seminary in Chicago, Illinois.

Sarah C. Kientz is a MDiv student at Vanderbilt Divinity School in Nashville, Tennessee.

Amy-Jill Levine is University Professor of New Testament and Jewish Studies, Mary Jane Werthan Professor of Jewish Studies, and Professor of New Testament Studies at Vanderbilt Divinity School and College of Arts and Science in Nashville, Tennessee.

Sarah McWhirt-Toler is a recent graduate of Vanderbilt Divinity School serving in children's ministry in Nashville, Tennessee.

Abby Mohaupt is a PhD student at Drew University, studying ecofeminist theology, trauma, and climate change; and a Presbyterian clergywoman who divides her time between El Granada, California, and Madison, New Jersey.

Anita Peebles is a MDiv student at Vanderbilt Divinity School and is pursuing ordination in the Alliance of Baptists.

Wes Pitts is Director of Christian Education at First Presbyterian Church in Statesville, North Carolina.

Anna Register is Children's Pastor at Gracepointe Church in Franklin, Tennessee.

Sandy Eisenberg Sasso is the Director of Religion, Spirituality and the Arts Initiative at Butler University and Christian Theological Seminary, and Rabbi Emerita of Congregation Beth-El Zedeck in Indianapolis, Indiana. She recently cofounded Women4Change Indiana.

Carol A. Wehrheim is an author, editor, curriculum consultant and Ruling Elder at Nassau Presbyterian Church in Princeton, New Jersey. She is a Distinguished Alumnus of McCormick Theological Seminary.

Alex Wirth is Associate Pastor at Lake View Presbyterian Church in Chicago, Illinois.

Luther Young Jr. is a MDiv student at Vanderbilt Divinity School and has worked as a Site Coordinator for the Nashville Freedom School Partnership, an initiative of the Children's Defense Fund.

Illustrators

Roberta Baird is a member of the Society of Children's Book Writers and Illustrators. Her work has been featured in magazines, books, and educational resources with clients such as Scholastic and McGraw-Hill. (104, 158, 170, 178, 254, 308, 322, 338)

Paige Billin-Frye has served as president and treasurer of the Children's Book Guild and was honored with her illustrations for *The House in the Meadow* being included in The Original Art Show at the Society of Illustrators in New York. (44, 100, 122, 174, 208, 224, 298, 320)

Kate Cosgrove is an illustrator and artist from Michigan. She received a BFA with honors from Michigan State University. Kate's illustrations have been published in all kinds of print and web media. (32, 70, 84, 120, 126, 226, 248, 262, 310)

Len Ebert is known for his easy, flowing lines and beautiful color. A skilled and versatile artist, he makes the driest subject interesting and does full justice to the lighthearted. (78, 200, 218, 252, 276)

Nell F. Fisher is a published illustrator of children's books and young adult books. (232, 266)

Laura Freeman received her BFA from the School of Visual Arts and began her career working for various editorial clients. She has illustrated over twenty children's books, including the Nikki and Deja series by Karen English. (16, 66, 108, 118, 128, 154, 216, 292, 314)

Darius Gilmont is an artist with many years of experience in educational illustration. Originally from England, he has lived in Israel since 1993, and the majority of his art, whether painting or sculpture, is on biblical, Old Testament themes. His work appeals to adults and children alike. Visit his website at www.darius-art.com. (22, 24, 26, 28, 36, 38, 40, 42, 52, 56, 92, 94)

Aimee Hagerty Johnson holds a BFA degree in Illustration from the Minneapolis College of Art and Design. Her hand-painted illustrations are often informed by literature, folk design, and her collection of vintage treasures. (82, 136, 146, 162, 176, 256, 316, 336)

Oksana Kemarskaya was born and raised in the Ukraine (formerly of the Soviet Union). Her education and drawing skills have deep roots from The Academic School of Russian Fine Art. Her passion to draw began when she was three years old. (76, 124, 172, 180, 220, 286, 290, 306, 326)

Art Kirchoff is an illustrator of children's books living in the St. Louis, Missouri, area. (90, 98, 240)

Laura Krushak-Tripp graduated with a BS degree in Art from Brigham Young University–Idaho where she focused on illustration. She loves creating illustrations of children and animals. (46, 88, 112, 140, 152, 204, 346)

Eleanor Troth Lewis is an illustrator of children's books and curriculum from Culpeper, Virginia. (50, 58, 64, 96, 110, 184, 190, 192, 194, 198, 202, 206, 210, 212, 214, 242, 270, 274, 324, 342)

Dennis McKinsey is an illustrator from Louisville, Kentucky. (334)

Nancy Munger graduated from the Art Center College of Design. She has been an illustrator for over forty years. Nancy specializes in traditional and digital illustrations for the children's book-publishing market. (60, 74, 244, 264, 268, 272, 282, 288, 300, 340)

Michelle Nidenoff is an illustrator and primarily illustrates children's books and educational materials. Michelle is also a skilled calligrapher, fine artist, and art instructor. She lives in Canada near Toronto. (166, 188, 260, 280, 302)

Craig Orback is a freelance children's book illustrator living near Seattle with his wife, Jessica, and son, Lewis. Since graduating with a BFA degree in Illustration from Cornish College of the Arts, he has illustrated over thirty children's books. Over the years, Craig has had the pleasure of working with clients including Scholastic Corp., Simon and Schuster, McGraw Hill, Lee & Low Books, Henry Holt, Millbrook Press, and Boys' Life. (30, 34, 48, 62, 106, 138, 160, 182, 186, 222, 234, 258, 278, 284, 294, 304, 312, 328)

Dani Padrón is a Spanish illustrator born in Galicia in 1983. He started his career in 2011, focusing on children's books, and has illustrated more than twenty titles since then. His work for "Pan de millo" (Kalandraka) was selected to participate in the Biennial of Illustration Bratislava 2015. (132, 134)

Lina Safar grew up in Kiev, Ukraine, and graduated with honors from the University of Damascus, Syria, School of Fine Arts. While studying, she began working in design, painting, and book illustration and has participated in many local and international exhibitions. (18, 20, 72, 144, 164, 296, 318, 332, 344)

Margaret Sanfilippo is an author and illustrator of children's and young adult books. (196, 230, 236, 250)

Gabhor Utomo received his degree from the Academy of Art University in San Francisco in 2003. His work has won numerous awards from local and national art organizations. His painting of Senator Milton Marks is a permanent collection at the California State Building in downtown San Francisco. (54, 68, 86, 102, 114, 130, 148, 246, 330)

Farida Zaman completed her art foundation course at Chelsea College of Art in London and graduated top of her class from London's Wimbledon School of Art. She is a member of the Society of Children's Book Writers and Illustrators, the Society of Illustrators in New York, the Graphic Artists Guild, and the Canadian Society of Children's Authors, Illustrators and Performers. (80, 116, 142, 150, 156, 168, 228, 238)

Scripture Index